TRANSPORT
THROUGH
THE AGES

uniform with this volume

ENGLISH ARCHITECTURE THROUGH THE AGES

Secular Building

Leonora and Walter Ison

BRITISH FURNITURE THROUGH THE AGES

illustrated by Maureen Stafford ARCA
edited with an introduction by
Robert Keith Middlemass

BRITISH DOMESTIC DESIGN THROUGH THE AGES

Brian Keogh and Melvyn Gill
edited with an introduction by
Robert Patterson

EUROPEAN INTERIOR DESIGN THROUGH THE AGES

illustrated by Anthony Sully
edited with an introduction by
Jeffery Daniels

TRANSPORT THROUGH THE AGES

Drawings by
BARBARA BROWN

Edited by

Peter Bray

ARTHUR BARKER LIMITED
5 Winsley Street London W1

Designed by Adrienne Kapadia
Printed by Unwin Bros
The Gresham press, Old Woking, Surrey
SBN 213 00248 5

Introduction

This collection of drawings has been designed to illustrate the story of transport from its beginnings to the present day. The introduction contains a brief history of transport linking together key developments which have taken place.

Early Man

From the earliest times ·men and women have sought the means of transporting themselves, materials, and goods, from place to place, and some far-reaching discoveries have been made, ranging from the wheel to the jet engine.

Primitive Man hunted on foot and carried the carcasses of dead animals over his shoulder. Later he used sledges made of flat pieces of wood or stone. Dogs were tamed to pull the sledges, and then log rollers were introduced and placed beneath the sledge, particularly for moving heavier loads.

When Man came into contact with water he used a floating log, to cling to or sit astride, but where there were no trees he was forced to use bundles of reeds or inflated animal skins.

The first boat as such was the dug-out canoe, and this was followed by the raft. Natives in the South Seas perfected the outrigger canoe. Other types of boat were the coracle and the kayak which were made of skin.

Asia and the Mediterranean c. 4000 BC – c. AD 400

The most important early advances in transportation were the taming of the horse and the invention of the wheel. The people of Central Asia tamed the wild horse. The wheel was probably used first in Mesopotamia about 4000 BC. Later it was introduced into the Far East and Egypt. In China and Persia there were some excellent highways for wheeled vehicles, but it was the Romans who brought road building to perfection.

The Egyptians were the pioneers of sea travel. When they began to trade with neighbouring countries, they constructed a specially strengthened form of ship which had been in use on the Nile for some years (figure 35). These ships developed into the war galleys of Phoenicia, Greece, and Rome and were all carvel-built (figure 37). The Phoenicians and Romans also built strong sailing ships.

In the Far East, the Chinese produced the first junks. They established a land route across Asia, and built canals to improve their internal communications.

The Northmen c. AD 400 – c. AD 1100

Remains found in Denmark and Norway show that the ships of Northern Europe were very different from the galleys and wheat ships of Rome. The Nydam boat (figure 52), and those found at Gokstad and Oseburg, were clinker-built (figure 56), and the Norman ships of 1066 were developed from these early Viking vessels.

The men from the North neglected the Roman roads, preferring instead to use tracks. Few bridges were built, and travellers relied on shallow fords for crossing streams. Carts, waggons and pack mules were used for transport.

By the 9th century AD, the first horse collar had appeared. The pulling power of horses was increased, but, in general, horses were smaller than those of later years.

The Middle Ages c. 1100 – c. 1400

Continued neglect of the roads retarded the development of land transport. Travellers experienced great difficulty when using wheeled vehicles, and merchants relied increasingly on the pack mule.

Travel in springless waggons was extremely uncomfortable, but in France some vehicles were built using leather straps as a form of suspension. In France, also, the breeding of stronger horses had very important consequences (figure 61).

More bridges were built during this period, and some famous examples still exist at Florence and Avignon (figures 63 and 67). The first London Bridge was completed in 1209.

Developments at sea led to the great voyages of the 15th and 16th centuries. In the Mediterranean, the evolution of the three-masted ship, incorporating the triangular lateen sail set fore and aft (figure 45), meant that the Arabs were well advanced in the art of sailing. In addition, they used the compass which came to them through contact with the Chinese.

European sailors still relied on the single square-rigged sail, using their ships for both warlike and peaceful purposes. When the vessels were required for fighting, temporary castles were fitted at the bow and stern. These castles gradually became a permanent feature of European ships. One important European development was the introduction of the stern rudder in the 12th and 13th centuries.

Canal building continued in China and Europe. It was on Italian canals in the 14th century that locks were first constructed to carry barges over rising ground.

The 15th, 16th and 17th Centuries

European ship designers had now reached a point where it was difficult to improve on their clinker-built, single-sail vessels. Contact with Arab nations brought about great changes, and encouraged by Henry the Navigator, a Portuguese prince, builders produced the three-masted carracks (figure 95) and caravels (figure 99) which took sailors to the Cape, India and America.

The increasing use of cannon tended to make ships unstable. In 1501, a Frenchman named Descharges introduced gun-ports which were cut in a ship's side. Guns could now be carried on lower decks, and as this innovation was better suited to carvel-built ships, the process of clinker building was gradually abandoned.

Several European nations built huge galleons in the first half of the 16th century. A typical example was the *Great Harry* of Henry VIII (figure 100). During this period the smaller three-masted ship developed sufficiently to allow Magellan (1519-22) and Drake (1577-80) to circumnavigate the world.

Some new developments appeared in the 17th century. In 1610 Phineas Pett built the *Royal Prince* (figure 106) which carried a fourth mast, and his *Sovereign of the Seas* (figure 109) was the first three-decker ever built. A great deal of decoration in the form of carvings and gilt figures was also a feature of these ships.

The condition of European roads continued to give cause for concern. Pack mules were in constant use, but at the beginning of the 16th century four-wheeled coaches were introduced in France, Holland, Italy and Spain. Important bridges were built, including Santa Trinita in Florence, the Ponte Rialto in Venice (figure 85) and the Pont Neuf in Paris.

In the 17th century more coaches came into use. Private owners kept them as a status symbol, but less wealthy people could now travel in stage coaches. In large towns hackney carriages and sedan chairs could be hired, and journeys became more comfortable when springs were fitted, towards the end of the century.

A significant new type of land transport appeared in Germany at the end of the

16th century. This was the wooden railed-way (figure 84), along which trucks were run to carry coal from the mines.

The 18th Century

In this century, road and canal systems in Europe were improved and extended, and as a result an increase in the speed of transport occurred towards 1800. On the Continent small, fast, private carriages became popular, and swift mail coaches were introduced in Britain in 1784. In France, the first attempts to harness steam to a road vehicle were made by Nicholas Cugnot in the 1760s (figure 132).

Wooden railed-ways became more numerous, and in 1767 the first metal rails were cast at Coalbrookdale in Shropshire. Richard Trevithick, working in Cornwall, built his first steam carriages at the end of the century.

At sea, the French, British and Dutch sailed two and three-decker heavily armed ships. *HMS Victory* (figure 152) is a typical vessel of this time. In America the emphasis was on faster vessels such as the frigate, brig and schooner.

The first steamboats were built in the 18th century. In 1737 a Gloucestershire man named Jonathan Hull experimented with a steam tug. Forty years later, in France, the Marquis de Jouffroy d'Abbans produced a paddle boat, and an American, John Fitch, built steamers in 1787 and 1790. Two Scotsmen, Patrick Miller and William Symington, also built a steam vessel in 1788 (figures 164-7).

One last development of the century was the first successful balloon flight. In Paris in 1783, two Frenchmen flew in a hot-air balloon made by the Montgolfier Brothers (figure 168). Later, another Frenchman reached a height of 10,000 feet in a hydrogen-filled balloon.

The 19th Century

In 1800 people were still travelling at speeds comparable with those of Roman times. By the end of the century, speeds of up to 100 m.p.h. were possible on land; sea transport had changed completely, and air travel was almost a reality.

Trevithick's early work with steam carriages reached fruition in 1804 when he ran a locomotive on rails at Merthyr Tydfil in Wales (figure 223). The world's first public railway was opened from Stockton to Darlington in 1825. In the USA the first line to exceed 100 miles in length was completed in 1833, and in 1869 a railway was laid across the American Continent. Railways spread to all parts of the world and competed strongly with roads for traffic and passengers.

Canals declined in the face of rail competition, but they developed in another direction. This was the ship canal. Ferdinand de Lesseps planned the Suez Canal, completed in 1869, and began work on the Panama Canal in 1888. The Corinth, Kiel and Manchester Ship Canals were opened in the 1890s.

During the first half of the century the use of steam instead of sail and the change-over from wooden to iron construction completely revolutionized shipping. In 1802 Symington built the *Charlotte Dundas,* usually regarded as the first successful steamboat. An American, Robert Fulton, in 1807 introduced the *Clermont* which began the world's first passenger services from New York to Albany (figures 251 and 252).

Following the Napoleonic Wars, services were opened across the Channel, and the first regular passages across the Atlantic were begun by Samuel Cunard in 1840. Iron built ships appeared in increasing numbers, and the paddle wheel was gradually replaced by the screw propeller.

Sailing ships had one last fling, monopolizing the route round the Cape, but when the Suez Canal was opened, steamers easily reached the Far East in a faster time. Compound engines and steel construction were further developments which sealed the fate of sailing ships.

The luxury liner appeared on the Atlantic run, and by 1900 German ships dominated this route. In 1897 Charles Parsons built a successful turbine-driven ship which produced very high speeds, and this engine was fitted to later vessels.

On European roads the disappearance of the coach was partly complemented by the introduction of the steam carriage and the bicycle, and later in the century the invention of the internal combustion engine led to the building of the first horseless carriages (figure 211). The horse-drawn bus, the tram, and the first underground railway also appeared in this century.

In 1852, Henri Giffard made the first powered airship flight in France (figure 279). Steam power was used but proved unsatisfactory. In 1884, Charles Renard and A. C. Krebs flew an electrically powered airship, but it was Count von Zeppelin's rigid airship of 1900 which proved the practicability of air travel.

The 20th Century

The earliest motor cars were very expensive, but in the USA Henry Ford produced cheaper models when he launched his *Model T* in 1909 (figure 286). Motoring now came within the reach of many more people.

The world's roads were not suited to the car, but the use of tar for road surfacing in Italy was quickly copied by other countries. The Italians, Germans, and Americans began building dual-carriageway arterial roads to link important centres, but town traffic the world over was becoming·increasingly congested. In spite of this, the convenience of road transport has undermined the world's railways, except in under-developed countries.

The railways have continued to decline, although electrification and diesel traction have been introduced. However, the Japanese have proved that the train is still an ideal form of inter-city communication with swift expresses travelling at over 100 m.p.h.

On the sea the turbine-powered *Mauretania* (figure 365), captured the Atlantic record in 1907. After World War I, European countries built giant liners like the *Normandie* and *Queen Mary* (figures 367 and 368), but rising costs made them uneconomical and they were replaced by the smaller *United States* and *Queen Elizabeth II* (figures 370 and 382). The modern giants are the 200,000 ton oil tankers.

The number of ship canals increased when the Panama Canal was opened in 1914. More recently the St Lawrence Seaway was completed in 1959.

The most far-reaching development of the 20th century has been the introduction of air travel. In 1910 the world's first airship passenger flights were made between Germany and Switzerland. During the next twenty-five years services were extended, but two tragic accidents to the *R101* (1930), and the *Hindenburg* (1937), gave impetus to the development of the aeroplane as a safer alternative.

Powered aeroplane flight began in 1903 when the Wright Brothers flew their first machine in the USA (figure 388). Technical advances, particularly during World War I, made possible two crossings of the Atlantic in 1919. In the same year commercial flights began between London and Paris, and the first regular Atlantic crossings were made in 1937.

During World War II the jet engine was successfully introduced and was later fitted to passenger aircraft. The first commercial jet aircraft was the *Comet I* of 1952. The latest jet airliners are capable of speeds of 600 m.p.h., and the Anglo-French *Concorde* will bring supersonic passenger travel in the 1970s (figure 410).

The helicopter, hovercraft and monorail have widened the scope of transport, but the most exciting developments have been the journeys of Russian and American astronauts into Space. Travel in the not-too-distant future may well be away from Earth altogether.

Early Man
LAND

1 MEN CARRYING CARCASE
When primitive men went hunting
they either dragged or carried the
dead animals back to their caves

2 PRIMITIVE SKIN SLEDGE
To ease the task of bringing home food, primitive men
produced the sledge. Some sledges, like the one above,
were made of skin

3 WOODEN SLEDGE
This was made of branches and was very difficult to pull
along

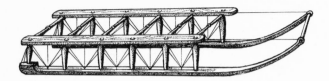

4 ARCTIC SLEDGE
The easiest sledge to use was that found in regions where there was snow and ice

5 Y-SLED PULLED BY DOG
Primitive men made a big step forward when they tamed animals to assist them. At first sledges were pulled by dogs, but later, other animals were used. The sledge above is made from a forked branch

6 LARGE EGYPTIAN SLEDGE
Before the wheel was introduced into Egypt, heavy loads, like the statue above, were transported on large sledges drawn by slaves

7 LOG ROLLERS
Friction between ground and sledge made transport very difficult, and in various parts of the world the log roller was developed successfully. Stonehenge must have been constructed with the help of roller transport

8 PERUVIAN ROPE BRIDGE

This simple method of crossing narrow gorges was used in the hilly regions of the world. The rope or cable was made of strong fibrous material

9 NEOLITHIC BRIDGE

Tarr Steps is situated in the West Country of England. It is thought to be 3,000 years old. The total length of the bridge is 140 feet, and it is 5 feet wide

10 PRIMITIVE BRIDGE

This ancient granite structure is also situated in the West of England. Four piers support three granite slabs, each 15 feet long

11 CHINESE SUSPENSION BRIDGE

This wonderful construction was made from bamboo saplings and lianas. It is known as the 'hammock' type. Bridges of this kind have been found in regions as far apart as Asia and South America

WATER

12 INFLATED SKINS — ASSYRIAN RELIEF
An inflated animal skin, used rather like a modern life jacket, was one method which was tried for crossing the rivers of Mesopotamia and Egypt

13 ASSYRIAN INFLATED SKIN RAFT
Inflated skins were sometimes bound together to form a raft. These were also used on the rivers of the Fertile Crescent, usually for transporting goods. They were called 'keleks'

14 A BARIS—EGYPTIAN REED RAFT
Where there were no suitable trees to use as floating logs or dug-outs, men lashed together papyrus reeds to form a raft

15 A HOLLOWED LOG
This craft was a development of the floating log which the earliest men sat astride. The cavity was either chipped out with an axe or hollowed out by fire

16 A SHAPED DUG-OUT CANOE
Men soon discovered how to manoeuvre this craft, and shaped the ends to gain additional speed. Many dug-outs are still used today in parts of Tropical Africa, New Guinea, and remote areas of Northern Australia

17 A CORACLE
An early British craft. A wickerwork frame was coated with pitch and then covered with hides. This craft can still be seen on some Welsh rivers

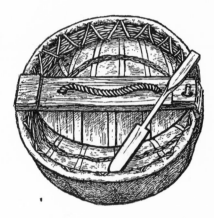

18 ESKIMO KAYAK
This canoe, for one person, is still used by Eskimos. Stretched skin covered the framework, leaving a central cockpit for the paddler. A larger version for several people was called an 'umiak'

19 A PACIFIC OUTRIGGER
The outrigger canoe was a development unknown in Europe. The boat, with a single boom, appeared in the Pacific, where it was ideal for negotiating the huge ocean rollers

20 FIJIAN OUTRIGGER CANOE
In some regions of the South Seas these boats were built up to a length of 100 feet. Some were fitted with a large triangular sail

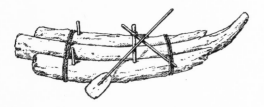

21 INDIAN CATAMARAN
The catamaran consisted of three logs lashed together to form a raft. They were used in coastal waters and on the rivers of India

22 A BRAZILIAN JANGADA
Rafts appear to have developed in the warmer areas of the world. One such vessel. which has survived to the present day, is the jangada of Brazil. This vessel was made of buoyant wood, probably balsa. It had a triangular sail and a shelter of matting was built amidships

Asia and the Mediterranean

LAND

23 WILD HORSE OF CENTRAL ASIA
The origins of the horse are somewhat obscure, but the wild horses of the steppe lands of Asia were the first to be tamed by Man. These horses were smaller than those of today, but once Man found a use for them, he made a momentous step forward in the development of transport

24 THE WHEEL
(a) *Tripartite Wheel* An early wheel made in three sections, and braced with ties held in place by copper nails. (b) *Later Wheel* Holes were made in the wheel to make it lighter. (c) *Spoked Wheel* Developed in the Middle East and used on chariots. It was stronger and lighter than earlier versions. (d) *Cross-bar Wheel* A strong heavy wheel used by the Greeks

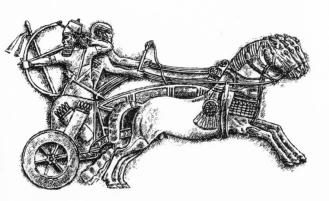

25 EASTERN OX-CART
Before the taming of the horse, the ox and ass had been used by Man. The picture shows a primitive ox-cart of the type used in the Far East, having a tripartite wheel and an axle fixed with wooden pegs

26 ASSYRIAN CHARIOT
The earliest chariots in Mesopotamia were built with solid wheels, but wall reliefs of about 2000 BC show chariots with spoked wheels. Later, these vehicles were used in Egypt where they became highly developed

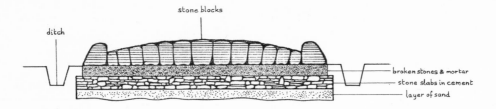

ditch

stone blocks

broken stones & mortar
stone slabs in cement
layer of sand

27 SECTION THROUGH A ROMAN ROAD

Although the civilisations of Mesopotamia and China used highways, it was the Romans who perfected the construction of roads. A good foundation and excellent drainage formed the basis of the road, while large stone blocks provided a smooth and durable surface

28 A STREET IN POMPEII

The excavation of this Roman town, destroyed in AD 79, has brought to light many interesting aspects of Roman life. The streets were rather narrow, paved with stone blocks, and edged with pavements. At intervals, stepping stones were laid for crossings. There was a gap between the stones to allow vehicle wheels to pass through

29 A ROMAN HORSEMAN

Although the Romans made great use of the horse, they sat astride without stirrups. These came to them from the Huns about AD 400

30 A ROMAN CART

The constant flow of trade throughout the Roman Empire relied on carts yoked to horses. The horse collar was unknown and, therefore, the horses took the weight of the load across their necks. This meant that heavy loads could not be moved without the greatest difficulty

31 A ROMAN CHARIOT
This chariot was a development of the types seen by the Romans in Egypt, Greece and Gaul. They were not often used in war, however, but they were used by messengers and important persons who wished to travel swiftly about the Empire. They were also used for racing. Again this vehicle was yoked to the horses

32 A CARPENTUM
A lady's chariot used in Roman times. It differed from the ordinary chariot in that a canopy was built above the carriage

33 ROMAN BRIDGE AT ALCANTARA, SPAIN
Some of the earliest Roman bridges were made of timber, but those built later were magnificent stone structures, like the one below built in AD 98 across the River Tagus. It has survived to the present day, towering 100 feet above the river, with its six huge arches made of granite

34 CAMEL CARAVAN
The Romans made contact with Eastern civilisations and trade routes were opened. The camel caravans from Eastern Asia brought fine silks to the Romans. This form of carrying merchandise survived well into modern times

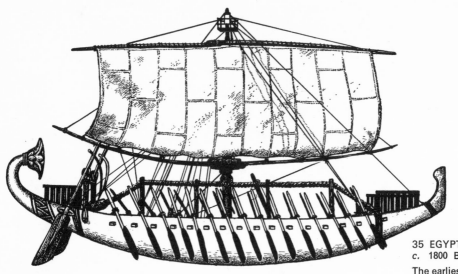

35 EGYPTIAN SHIP
c. 1800 BC
The earliest Egyptian ships were made of short planks and were carvel-built (see figure 37). They were used only on the River Nile. About 3000 BC the Egyptians took to the sea to trade with their neighbours. The ships were considerably strengthened, a strong rope truss being stretched over props, and running from bow to stern. They were propelled by oars and a single sail which was collapsible. Steering was by means of two oars at the rear of the ship

36 EGYPTIAN SHIP
c. 1300 BC
Pictures of later ships show that a keel plank running the length of the ship, and projecting fore and aft, had now come into use. However, the rope truss was still very much in evidence. The vessel was probably about 80 feet long

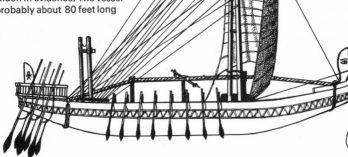

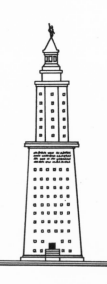

37 DIAGRAM SHOWING CARVEL CONSTRUCTION
In carvel building the planks of the hull are butted edge to edge and the frame and keel provide the strength to withstand the sea. This type of construction was used by all Mediterranean nations

38 THE PHAROS AT ALEXANDRIA
One of the Seven Wonders of the World, this huge lighthouse, said to have been 600 feet high, was built on a small island at Alexandria. It was built by Sostratus in the third century BC, but was destroyed by an earthquake in the thirteenth century

39 PHOENICIAN SHIP
c. 1300 BC
This was very similar to the
Egyptian ship of this period, but
was obviously strong enough to
withstand the sea without a rope
truss to support the hull. It was a
merchant ship using sail only

40 PHOENICIAN SHIP
c. 800 BC
A sturdy construction, using long
planks for the hull. Oars as well as
sails were used for propulsion.
The rope ladder and mast top are
notable innovations

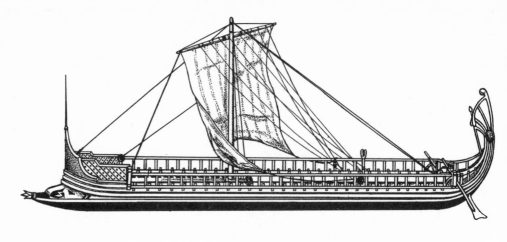

41 GREEK WAR GALLEY 500 BC
The emphasis here was on manoeuvrability, speed and strength. A strong keel ran the length of the ship, and at the bow was a large ram and a fighting bridge for soldiers. Oars, arranged in banks, were operated by slaves, although there was a single sail. The 'bireme', a galley with double banks of oars, was the type most commonly used

42 JUDAEAN SHIP c. 300 BC
A merchant ship notable for a sail arrangement which appears to be moving away from the square-rigged sail to a sail rigged fore and aft

43 ROMAN GALLEY
Built to fight against the Carthaginians. It was very similar to the Greek galley, but some vase paintings show a fighting tower placed amidships

44 ROMAN CARGO SHIP AD 200

These broad corn carrying vessels were built with stern-posts shaped like the neck of a swan. Either side of this the wide deck made room for two steering oars. The ship had a central square sail, but at the bow was a second mast, angled forward, which carried another sail called an 'artemon'

45 AN ARAB SAMBUK

This belongs to a group of sailing ships known as *dhows*. It was flat-sterned and carried triangular 'lateen' sails running fore and aft. These sails were now coming into use in the Mediterranean area. They gave greater manoeuvrability and were copied many years later by European ship builders. The vessel above is a modern type of sambuk using a stern rudder, not steering oars

The Northmen
LAND

46 SLEDGE FROM THE OSEBURG SHIP
This elaborate sledge was found in the Oseburg burial mound in 1903. While it was only intended for ceremonial purposes, it does show that this type of vehicle was still in use in northern lands where there was snow and ice

47 CART FROM THE OSEBURG SHIP
Again a ceremonial vehicle, but its importance lies in that it shows the cart being used in Northern Europe at this date, probably in lowland areas

48 OX-DRAWN CART
These vehicles were in fairly common use in Southern Europe, particularly for hauling heavier loads. The oxen were yoked to the cart

49 A HORSE-DRAWN DRAY
The horse collar appeared in about the ninth century. This enabled the horse to use its strong shoulders for pulling carts

50 PILLION RIDING
A method of travel favoured through the centuries, enabling two persons to ride the same horse

WATER

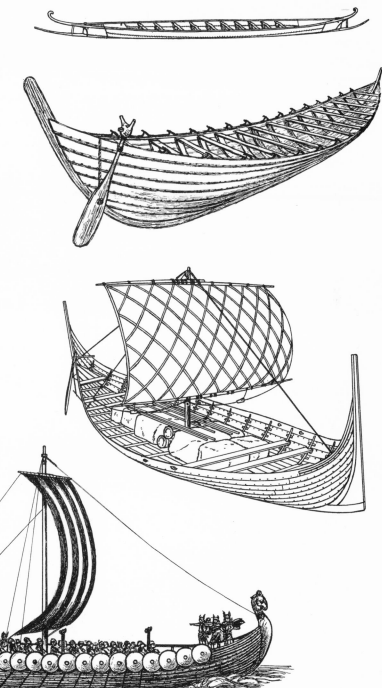

51 THE HJORTSPRING BOAT
c. 200 BC
The earliest wooden Scandinavian boat yet discovered. In appearance it is very similar to the hide canoe. It was over 40 feet long and 6 feet wide

52 THE NYDAM BOAT
c. AD 300
Discovered in 1863. It was made of oak and was clinker-built (see figure 56), unlike Mediterranean ships. It was propelled by oars and was 75 feet long

53 SCANDINAVIAN MERCHANT SHIP
AD 800–900
This ship had an open hull and the cargo rested on the bottom. A small number of oarsmen, helped by a single sail, propelled the boat along. A single rudder oar was placed at the rear of the ship on the 'steerboard' side

54 THE GOKSTAD SHIP
NINTH CENTURY AD
Discovered in Norway in 1886. It was 76 feet long and 17 feet broad amidships. Thirty-two oarsmen propelled the ship, and there was a strong central mast which carried a single sail

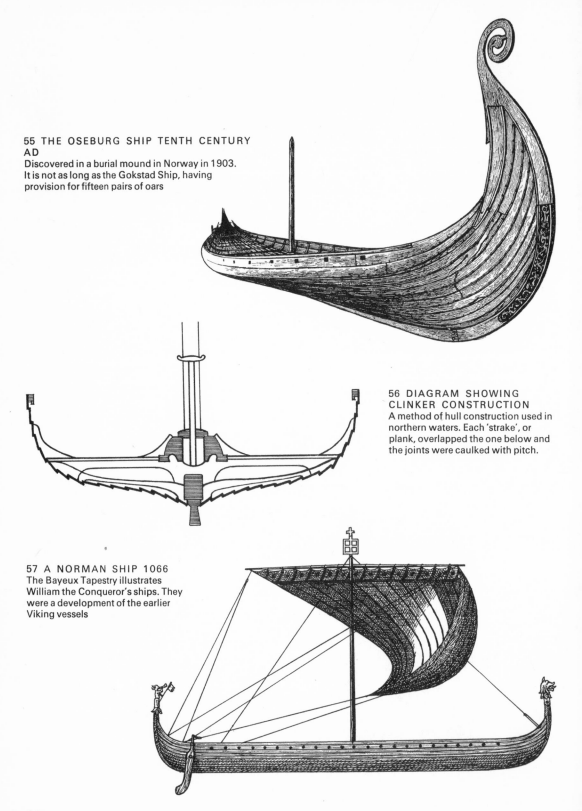

55 THE OSEBURG SHIP TENTH CENTURY AD
Discovered in a burial mound in Norway in 1903.
It is not as long as the Gokstad Ship, having
provision for fifteen pairs of oars

56 DIAGRAM SHOWING CLINKER CONSTRUCTION
A method of hull construction used in
northern waters. Each 'strake', or
plank, overlapped the one below and
the joints were caulked with pitch.

57 A NORMAN SHIP 1066
The Bayeux Tapestry illustrates
William the Conqueror's ships. They
were a development of the earlier
Viking vessels

The Middle Ages
LAND

58 PACK MULE
Most light goods were carried by strings of pack mules. The merchandise was carried in panniers slung on either side of the animal

59 BAND OF PILGRIMS
These groups of people, on horseback or on foot, were a common sight in Europe as they journeyed to visit the shrines of famous saints

60 HORSE-DRAWN CART
Poor roads were a constant hazard to wheeled vehicles. The cart below is fitted with studded wheels to combat this

61 A SHIRE HORSE
This breed of large horse came from France. It was used by both knights and farmers

62 LONG-WAGGON OR WHIRLICOTE
Generally used by women of noble birth, along with the horse-drawn litter. It was perhaps the most comfortable form of travel of the period

25

63 BRIDGE AT AVIGNON, FRANCE
St. Bénezèt built this beautiful arched
bridge across the Rhône at Avignon
between 1178 and 1188

**64 THE MONNOW BRIDGE,
WALES**
This bridge at Monmouth dates from
the thirteenth century. It is the only
bridge in Britain which still has a
fortified tower on the bridge itself.
Triangular 'cutwaters' can be seen
on the arches

**65 THE HUNTINGDON BRIDGE,
ENGLAND**
Dating from about 1300, this bridge is
interesting because it appears to have
been built by two groups of people
working from opposite banks. The
piers on the left are triangular, whereas
those on the right are semi-hexagonal

**66 SERCHIO BRIDGE, LUCCA,
ITALY**
An arched bridge built across the River
Serchio in 1317. The large centre arch
has a span of 120 feet and the road
on top is 12 feet wide. The bridge is
well founded, having withstood the
severe flooding of the river for over
600 years

**67 PONTE VECCHIO,
FLORENCE, ITALY**
This bridge crosses the River
Arno in Florence. It was the first
to be constructed using segmental
curves for bridge arches. Shops
line either side of the bridge

WATER

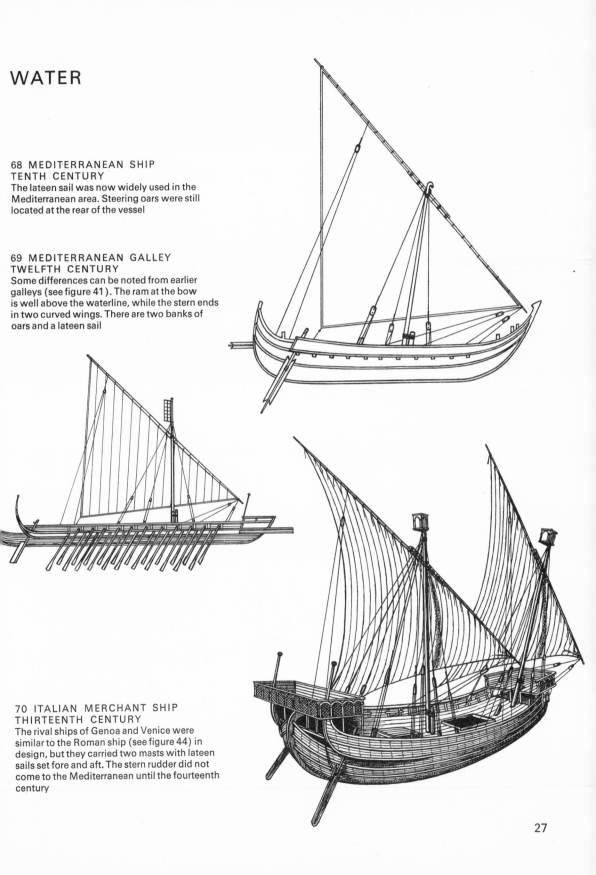

**68 MEDITERRANEAN SHIP
TENTH CENTURY**
The lateen sail was now widely used in the
Mediterranean area. Steering oars were still
located at the rear of the vessel

**69 MEDITERRANEAN GALLEY
TWELFTH CENTURY**
Some differences can be noted from earlier
galleys (see figure 41). The ram at the bow
is well above the waterline, while the stern ends
in two curved wings. There are two banks of
oars and a lateen sail

**70 ITALIAN MERCHANT SHIP
THIRTEENTH CENTURY**
The rival ships of Genoa and Venice were
similar to the Roman ship (see figure 44) in
design, but they carried two masts with lateen
sails set fore and aft. The stern rudder did not
come to the Mediterranean until the fourteenth
century

27

**71 SWEDISH COASTAL VESSEL
THIRTEENTH CENTURY**
A small clinker-built vessel made of oak. There are small decks at bow and stern, and cross beams amidships to strengthen the hull

**72 SHIP OF THE CINQUE PORTS
THIRTEENTH CENTURY**
The Cinque Ports on the south coast of England ran broad vessels which now carried castles at bow and stern. The long bowsprit was also a prominent feature of these ships

**73 SHIP OF THE THIRTEENTH CENTURY
WITH STERN RUDDER**
Pictures from Sweden, and port seals from England and France dating from the twelfth and thirteenth centuries, show that the stern rudder had begun to take the place of the steering oar. Above is a small Swedish ship showing this new feature

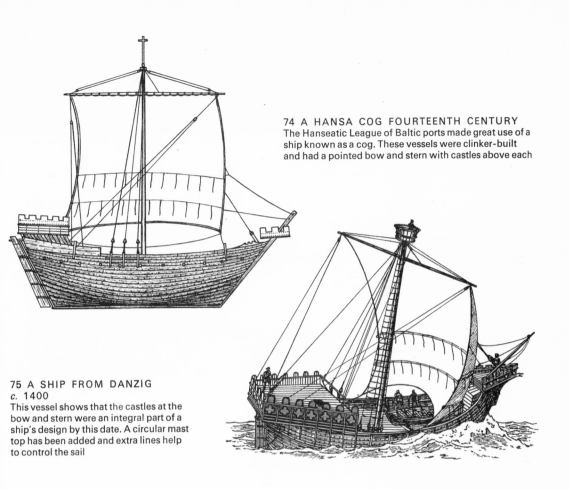

74 A HANSA COG FOURTEENTH CENTURY
The Hanseatic League of Baltic ports made great use of a
ship known as a cog. These vessels were clinker-built
and had a pointed bow and stern with castles above each

75 A SHIP FROM DANZIG
c. 1400
This vessel shows that the castles at the
bow and stern were an integral part of a
ship's design by this date. A circular mast
top has been added and extra lines help
to control the sail

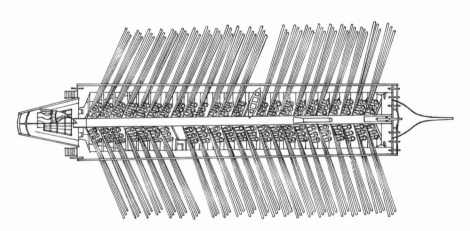

76 PLAN OF A MEDITERRANEAN GALLEY *c.* 1400
A plan view of the ship shows the oars worked *alla sensile,* that is, arranged
in groups of three on one level with one man per oar

77 CHINESE MARINER'S COMPASS
The Chinese are thought to have developed a mariner's compass towards the end of the thirteenth century. They took the distinguishing mark of the instrument as South, and marked off twenty-four points. A sensitive needle one inch long was pivoted to point out the markings

78 A SAMPAN
A light craft used on rivers and in coastal waters in the Far East. The modern versions usually have an awning of matting towards the stern. The boat is propelled along by a single scull placed over the stern

79 FOOCHOW JUNK
This type of junk was carvel-built, and the strong frame and bulkheads formed the hull into a series of watertight compartments. The foremast and mizzenmast were located at the extreme ends of the ship

80 ANTUNG JUNK
Different from the junks of Southern China. The hull was strong and had a flat bottom with no keel. To offset this, a large rudder was added to prevent drift. Four masts, including two mizzen masts, were fitted, and the sails were not supported by stays

The 15th, 16th and 17th Centuries

LAND

81 ITALIAN LITTER
SIXTEENTH CENTURY
This was the forerunner of the Sedan Chair, and was popular on the Continent of Europe among wealthy ladies. It was a small carriage slung between poles, and carried by servants

82 A WHIRLICOTE
A development of earlier models. It was still a springless vehicle used mostly by ladies, but it was sometimes used for hire in the manner of a hackney coach

83 TUDOR COACHES
Coaches were introduced into England from the Continent in the 1560s. Some were uncomfortable and springless, like those above, but others were suspended on leather straps, an idea taken from France

84 EARLY MINING TRUCK
These first appeared near mines in Germany at the end of the sixteenth century. The miners pushed the trucks along wooden rails

85 PONTE RIALTO, VENICE, ITALY
Built over the Grand Canal in Venice between 1587 and 1591. One segmental arch spans the Canal, and an arcade of thirteen arches supports the roof. The bridge is lined with shops

86 COACH OF HENRY IV OF FRANCE, 1610
Coaches were still comparatively rare in Paris at this time. The king's coach was square-shaped with a canopy set over four wheels. Elaborate colour and decoration was used on the body and tapestries

87 OLD LONDON BRIDGE IN 1616
The only bridge across the Thames in London until the eighteenth century. First built in the thirteenth century, but houses and shops were added in succeeding years. It became a focal point of trade in the capital. The low arches prevented sea-going ships from proceeding any further up river

88 COACH OF THE REIGN OF CHARLES II
A mourning coach of the late seventeenth century. Slung on leather straps, it was a rather cumbersome vehicle

89 ENGLISH LIGHT COACH
LATE SEVENTEENTH CENTURY
This light coach ,or chariot, was developed in the late seventeenth century. The leather decoration was very elaborate. Springing consisted of strong leather straps suspended from the upper cross bars of the frame

90 SUSPENSION DIAGRAMS
a. Leather strap suspension used in the sixteenth and seventeenth centuries. b. The first springs were used towards the end of the seventeenth century. They were made in the form of a 'C'. This helped to make coaches faster and more comfortable

91 A FRENCH BROUETTE
A private carriage for two people which was very popular in France. However, they were somewhat unstable, and were liable to overturn if driven too fast

92 A FRENCH VINAIGRETTE LATE SEVENTEENTH CENTURY
This carriage, mounted on two wheels, was pulled along by a man and pushed from the rear by a woman or child. Entrance to the cab was by means of a door at the front, between the shafts

93 AN ENGLISH PHAETON 1698
A fast vehicle designed for two people

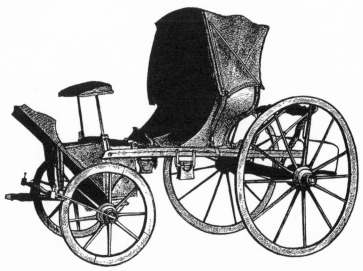

WATER

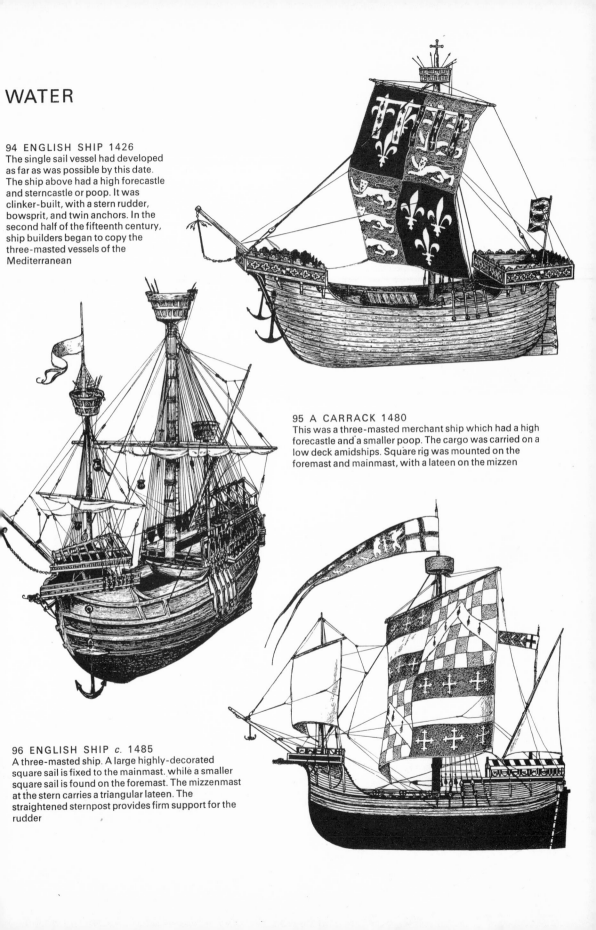

94 ENGLISH SHIP 1426
The single sail vessel had developed as far as was possible by this date. The ship above had a high forecastle and sterncastle or poop. It was clinker-built, with a stern rudder, bowsprit, and twin anchors. In the second half of the fifteenth century, ship builders began to copy the three-masted vessels of the Mediterranean

95 A CARRACK 1480
This was a three-masted merchant ship which had a high forecastle and a smaller poop. The cargo was carried on a low deck amidships. Square rig was mounted on the foremast and mainmast, with a lateen on the mizzen

96 ENGLISH SHIP c. 1485
A three-masted ship. A large highly-decorated square sail is fixed to the mainmast. while a smaller square sail is found on the foremast. The mizzenmast at the stern carries a triangular lateen. The straightened sternpost provides firm support for the rudder

97 VENETIAN GONDOLA LATE FIFTEENTH CENTURY

This slim boat was, and still is, used on the canals of Venice. Some were privately owned, others could be hired. The long oar at the rear fits into a fork-shaped bracket. The gondolier stands up to propel the boat

98 THE *SANTA MARIA* 1492

No absolutely certain picture of this ship has come down to us. Experts agree she was probably a carrack. From Columbus' log we know she carried a mainsail, topsail, foresail, spritsail, and a lateen mizzen sail. She was probably about 90 feet long

99 PORTUGUESE CARAVEL 1535

The caravel was a sleek vessel having a shallow draught. It was faster than a carrack. Most caravels were fitted with two or three masts rigged with lateen sails. The hull was unusually low for vessels of this period

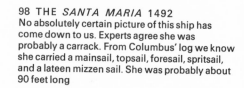

100 THE *GREAT HARRY* 1540

Built in 1514, but extensively refitted some 26 years later. She carried a fourth mast at the rear known as the 'bonaventure'. Her masts were rigged not only for topsails above the mainsails, but for topgallants also. She was flat-sterned and had a high forecastle projecting over the bows. The six decks aft of the mainmast carried up to 150 guns

101 VENETIAN TRIREME *c.* 1540
Driven by three banks of oars and having a
raised bridge in the stern. One mast carried
a sail, although it is known that some
galleys did have three sails

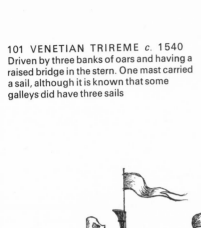

102 NEAPOLITAN GALEASS 1583
This was a galleon which also used oars for
propulsion. The object of the design was to have
the strength of a heavy ship, and at the same time
have manoeuvrability when there was no wind.
A heavy reinforced ram was carried on the bow
of this high-sided vessel

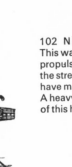

103 A DUTCH GALLEON 1590
A three-masted ship very similar to the
English type. The poop was high, but
the forecastle was low with part,
known as the beak, jutting out over the
water and supporting a bowsprit

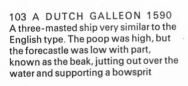

104 AN ENGLISH GALLEON LATE FIFTEENTH CENTURY

Reliable information is scarce about this type of vessel, but it appears to have been constructed with an eye to seaworthiness and manoeuvrability. The high castles and extensive rig found on the *Great Harry* were greatly reduced, but the long beak of the kind found on Dutch ships projected well beyond the bow

105 WHIPSTAFF

This steering lever guided the rudder, and in the sixteenth century a whipstaff was designed like the one below, where the helmsman could observe the sails while steering

106 THE *ROYAL PRINCE* 1610

Built by Phineas Pett for James I of England. She was a four-master carrying extra sail. There was a row of windows in the stern galleries, and a good deal of decoration in the form of plumes and coats-of-arms. She weighed 1,200 tons and was 130 feet long

107 EAST INDIAMAN 1612
The British East India Company was founded in 1600.
The Company's vessels, built at Deptford, were squat and
cumbersome, carrying four masts and rather too much
canvas. They were heavily armed against pirates

108 THE *MAYFLOWER* 1620
No drawings of this famous ship have survived
to the present day, but models have been
constructed using the available evidence.
She was a three-master having main and
topsails on the mainmast and foremast. A
lateen was fixed to the mizzen

**109 THE *SOVEREIGN OF
THE SEAS* 1637**
Designed by Phineas Pett, this
vessel was one of the first to be
built from the Ship Money collected
by order of Charles I. She was the
first three-decker ever built, and the
tall masts carried royal sails above
the topgallants. Pett incorporated a
round stern into the ship's design
(see figure 110), and he made
her into the most decorated ship of
the period with gilt figures, coats-
of-arms, and monograms

110 DIAGRAM SHOWING 'ROUND-TUCK' STERN
An innovation on seventeenth century British ships. The stern planks were rounded up from the waterline before the upper part of the stern was squared off. This method of construction helped to prevent drag through the water. Continental builders still used the square transom stern

111 ENGLISH WARSHIP 1675
A typical heavy deep-going ship. She was a three-decker used in line of battle, and could carry 100 guns. Heavy decoration is still evident, but the high poops and forecastles are showing signs of levelling out

112 DUTCH YACHT 1680
The Dutch yacht, or jacht, was originally a small swift sailing vessel. The single-masted ship was used for scouting and convoy work. and also for carrying people of importance. Rigging was set fore and aft, and the leeboards at the side of the hull enabled the ship to beat to windward

113 THE *ROYAL ESCAPE*
Prince Charles, later Charles II, escaped to France in this ship after his defeat at Worcester in 1651. It remained in his service as a yacht until 1672

114 THE *BRITANNIA* 1682

The largest ship built since the *Sovereign of the Seas*. She was fitted with three masts and an elaborately curved beak. Her designation by the Admiralty was as a 'first-rate', that is, a ship carrying over 100 guns

115 WINSTANLEY'S EDDYSTONE LIGHTHOUSE LATE 1690s

Henry Winstanley built this lighthouse, the first in England, on Eddystone Rock near Plymouth. It was destroyed in a storm in 1703, and Winstanley was killed in the disaster

116 AN IRISH CURRAGH *c.* 1685

This was a very strong hide boat. She was used in Irish coastal waters, and was capable of standing up to rough seas and breakers

117 RIVER CRAFT LATE SEVENTEENTH CENTURY

A collection of craft that could be seen on the Thames. The rowing boat was probably engaged on naval business, while the yacht-like vessels would be either coal or merchandise carriers

The 18th Century
LAND

118 CAUSEY ARCH, ENGLAND 1727
The earliest known railway bridge. It was built in County Durham to carry a waggon way over Causey Burn

119 WADE'S BRIDGE AT ABERFELDY, SCOTLAND 1733
General Wade superintended the building of military roads in Scotland, and this bridge, with its five arches, remains as a monument to his productive work

120 IRON BRIDGE NEAR COALBROOKDALE, ENGLAND 1777
This was the first iron bridge built in Europe. Abraham Darby and John Wilkinson were responsible for its construction between 1777 and 1779. The arch had a span of 100 feet, and the bridge gave the name of Ironbridge to the town which it served.

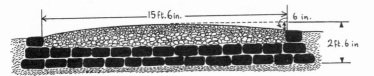

121 SECTION THROUGH A FRENCH ROAD *c.* 1750

Roads in France in the mid-eighteenth century were the best in Europe, largely due to the work of Tresaquet. A solid foundation formed the basis of the three-layer construction, and a well-curved camber allowed for good drainage. Tresaquet employed a force of paid labourers to keep up road repair

122 TELFORD ROAD SECTION *c.* 1800

Thomas Telford's precise specifications for road construction made his roads very costly. He relied on very firm foundations, with two layers of carefully chosen bricks of special size and weight. A layer of gravel on the surface was one inch thick, and a six-inch camber meant that drainage was good.

123 HEAVY WAGGON MID-EIGHTEENTH CENTURY

These cumbersome vehicles travelled only a few miles per day. Several laws were passed forcing waggon owners to fit wider wheels to help combat road damage. The waggon above would have 16-inch wheel rims

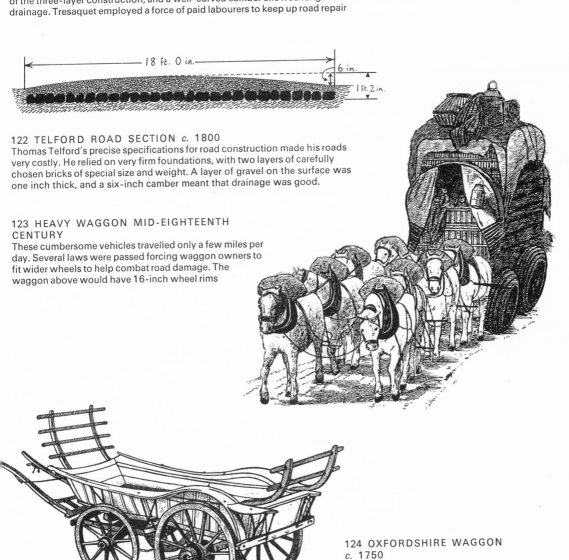

124 OXFORDSHIRE WAGGON *c.* 1750

A vehicle in common use during the eighteenth century for carrying produce to the farmhouse or into town

125 TOLLHOUSE

The turnpike system in Britain necessitated the collection of tolls. Tollhouses were built so that these collections could be made at specific points. The buildings were often octagonal in shape with the windows situated in such a way that the toll-keeper had a clear view up and down the road

126 ENGLISH POST CHAISE 1725

A fast covered coach, much favoured by private owners. The driver did not drive from the carriage but took the postillion position on one of the horses

127 FRENCH CABRIOLET 1750

This was a light conveyance for one person. It was drawn by one horse and was very popular with the fashionable young men of the period

128 FRENCH TOWN AND COUNTRY BERLIN
c. 1770

These stable coaches were used by fashionable ladies in French cities. The body was mounted on two shafts and set high off the road. Suspension was in the form of 'C' springs. They were very comfortable and suitable for long distance travel

129 FRENCH VIS-A-VIS 1775
This name was given to a light carriage, drawn by one horse, which carried two passengers who sat facing each other in single seats

130 SEDAN CHAIR 1770
A similar model to the litter of earlier centuries. This form of transport originated in France. The vehicle was used mainly by ladies of wealth and was usually carried by footmen

131 ENGLISH MAIL COACH 1784
John Palmer of Bath introduced these fast coaches on to English roads. They were well guarded against highway robbery. The first coach ran from London to Bath in 1784, and other services followed quickly to other parts of the country

132 CUGNOT'S STEAM CARRIAGE 1769
In Paris in the 1760s, Nicholas Cugnot built the first self-propelled vehicle. It was a three-wheeled carriage on a heavy chassis, carrying a large steam boiler at the front. An unfortunate accident discouraged Cugnot from continuing with his work

**133 THE CANAL BASIN AT
WORSLEY, MANCHESTER 1759**
The Bridgewater Canal, designed by
James Brindley, was the first modern
canal built in Britain. It ran for a distance of
about 10 miles, and was constructed to
carry coal into Manchester because the
roads were so poor. The basin at Worsley
shows the tunnel built into the entrance
of the mine

**134 BARTON AQUEDUCT ON
THE BRIDGEWATER CANAL
1761**
This was a wonderful feat of
engineering by Brindley to carry the
canal over the River Irwell. Stone,
lined with clay, was used in its
construction, and the centre arch had a
span of 63 feet

**135 THE TRENT AND MERSEY CANAL AT ETRURIA,
STAFFORDSHIRE 1777**
Brindley planned this great project which was completed five years after his
death. Josiah Wedgwood, the pottery manufacturer, needed this new form
of transport to carry his delicate commodity to the ports. The horse-drawn
barges were quicker and safer than carts on the roads, but not always cheaper

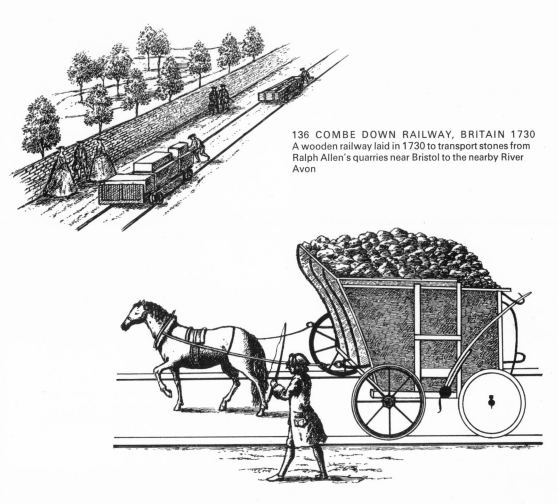

136 COMBE DOWN RAILWAY, BRITAIN 1730
A wooden railway laid in 1730 to transport stones from
Ralph Allen's quarries near Bristol to the nearby River
Avon

137 HORSE-DRAWN WAGGON WAY
Towards the end of the eighteenth century, iron rails and flanged wheels came
into use. Stronger trucks could now be made and more coal carried. These
trucks were usually horse-drawn

**138 TRUCK FROM THE COMBE
DOWN RAILWAY 1730**
These small trucks were used on Ralph
Allen's quarry railway. The wooden rails
and pegs were constantly breaking under
the trucks' weight

WATER

139 BRITISH ROAL YACHT *c.* 1712
An elaborately equipped royal ship used in the early eighteenth century

140 A DUTCH FLUYT *c.* 1700
A Dutch merchantman which had a round stern and was flat-bottomed.
Originally these vessels were rather narrow, but by 1700 broader
decks were more common

141 ENGLISH WARSHIP 1706
A 'second rate' of 90 guns built to Admiralty
specifications as laid down in 1706. The
stern galleries show balconies which were
attached to the cabins of senior officers.
The ship weighed 1,550 tons

142 A 50 GUN SHIP *c.* 1736
One of a squadron which sailed round the world under Admiral Anson. She was a two-decker with a poop, and was particularly suitable for long cruises. She weighed 853 tons

143 NEWCASTLE BARK *c.* 1750
The many different types of merchantmen of this period were classified by the construction of their hull rather than by their rig. The bark had no beak head and was blunt at the bow. It was capable of carrying a frigate rig

144 A MEDITERRANEAN POLACCA
c. 1750
This name was given to a large two or three-masted vessel with a square rig. Polacre was an alternative name which was used

145 LONDON COMPANY BARGE
c. 1750
Used on the Thames in the eighteenth century when the Lord Mayor's procession was held on the River. This barge, belonging to the Worshipful Company of Shipwrights, has an ark built towards the stern

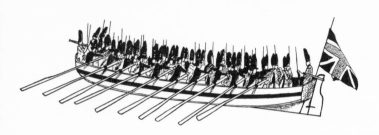

146 LANDING CRAFT *c.* 1759
The type used by Wolfe's troops at Quebec in 1759. These boats could be dismantled and stored in a ship's hold

147 EIGHTEENTH CENTURY MIDSHIP SECTIONS
These diagrams show the mid-sections of various two-deckers about 1750. (a) English (b) Dutch (c) French

148 THAMES BARGE *c.* 1760
A small coastal vessel with a yacht-like rig. Probably used to carry coal

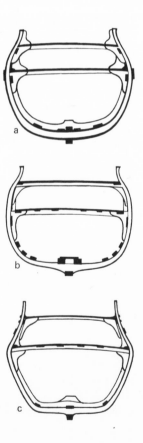

149 MEDITERRANEAN CHEBEC *c.* **1760**
Used by Mediterranean nations and by Barbary pirates.
The ship had a shallow draught, and was rigged with
lateen sails. The hull was slim with a pointed beak head at
the bow and a projecting deck at the stern. She could
carry up to 28 guns

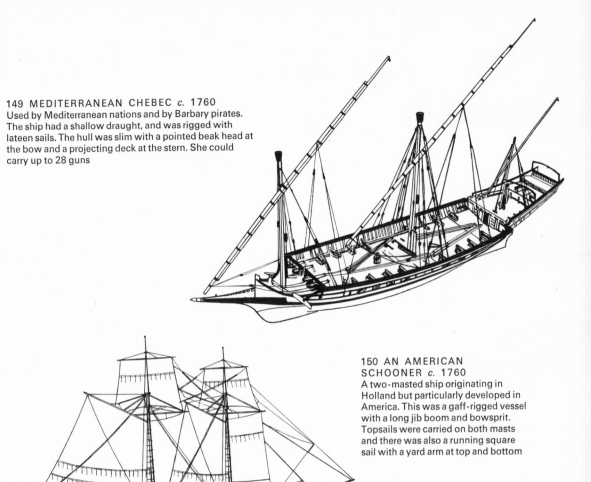

**150 AN AMERICAN
SCHOONER** *c.* **1760**
A two-masted ship originating in
Holland but particularly developed in
America. This was a gaff-rigged vessel
with a long jib boom and bowsprit.
Topsails were carried on both masts
and there was also a running square
sail with a yard arm at top and bottom

151 A 60 GUN SHIP 1757
The *Achilles,* a typical 60 gun ship of the period, built at Harwich. She was a
two-decker, but the poop and forecastle were longer than hitherto

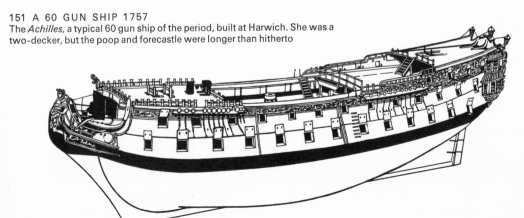

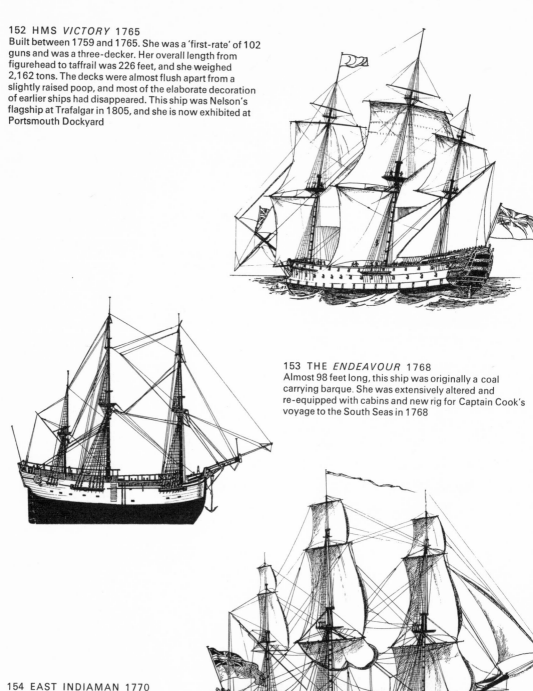

152 HMS *VICTORY* 1765
Built between 1759 and 1765. She was a 'first-rate' of 102
guns and was a three-decker. Her overall length from
figurehead to taffrail was 226 feet, and she weighed
2,162 tons. The decks were almost flush apart from a
slightly raised poop, and most of the elaborate decoration
of earlier ships had disappeared. This ship was Nelson's
flagship at Trafalgar in 1805, and she is now exhibited at
Portsmouth Dockyard

153 THE *ENDEAVOUR* 1768
Almost 98 feet long, this ship was originally a coal
carrying barque. She was extensively altered and
re-equipped with cabins and new rig for Captain Cook's
voyage to the South Seas in 1768

154 EAST INDIAMAN 1770
Built of teak with good quarters for
passengers and crew. Numerous guns
were carried for defence. She weighed
864 tons and was particularly large for
her day

155 EAST INDIAMAN 1797
This heavily-armed ship, the *Warley*, was in service until 1809. In 1804 she drove off a French squadron in the Indian Ocean and saved a very valuable cargo

156 AN AMERICAN FRIGATE 1790s
The American style of frigate was probably the finest ever built and was generally larger than the corresponding European type. She was well armed with over 40 guns, and was rigged with skysails above the royals. These helped to give a speed of 15 knots

157 ENGLISH FRIGATE 1796
A 32 gun vessel. In the Navy she was used as a swift scouting and convoy ship. She was a strong all-weather ship, flat-sterned, but rigged with far less sail than the American type

158 A BRIG LATE EIGHTEENTH CENTURY

Developed from the smaller brigantine. The vessel was two-masted, rigged with square sails, and topgallants above the main and topsails. Sometimes these ships were high-rigged with royals. The brigsail was latched to a spar aft of the mainmast

159 BALTIMORE CLIPPER LATE EIGHTEENTH CENTURY

This was the forerunner of the great clipper ships of the nineteenth century, although much smaller. She was a very swift vessel with sharp bows and rigged like a schooner

160 EUROPEAN MERCHANTMAN 1800

Vessels of this type were common in European waters by 1800. They were square-rigged on all masts, and carried spritsails on a long bowsprit

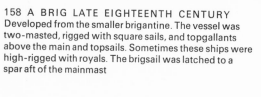

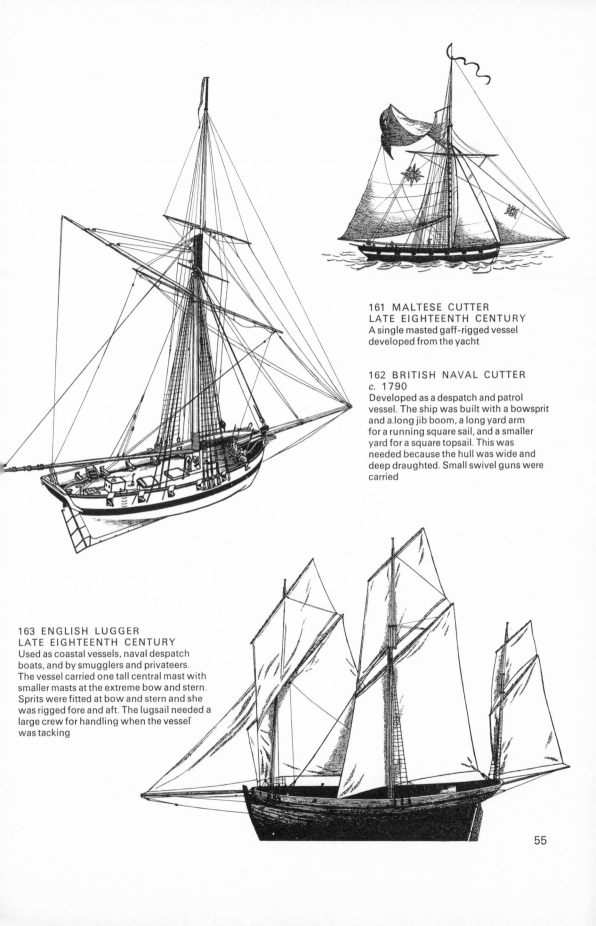

**161 MALTESE CUTTER
LATE EIGHTEENTH CENTURY**
A single masted gaff-rigged vessel
developed from the yacht

162 BRITISH NAVAL CUTTER
c. 1790
Developed as a despatch and patrol
vessel. The ship was built with a bowsprit
and a long jib boom, a long yard arm
for a running square sail, and a smaller
yard for a square topsail. This was
needed because the hull was wide and
deep draughted. Small swivel guns were
carried

**163 ENGLISH LUGGER
LATE EIGHTEENTH CENTURY**
Used as coastal vessels, naval despatch
boats, and by smugglers and privateers.
The vessel carried one tall central mast with
smaller masts at the extreme bow and stern.
Sprits were fitted at bow and stern and she
was rigged fore and aft. The lugsail needed a
large crew for handling when the vessel
was tacking

164 HULL'S STEAM TUG 1737

The tug was powered by a Newcomen engine driving stern paddle wheels. The boat was apparently tried out on the River Avon in Gloucestershire, but not developed

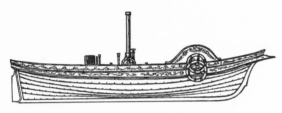

165 THE *PYROSCAPHE* 1783

Built by the Marquis Claude de Jouffroy d'Abbans and sailed on the River Saône near Lyons. Paddle wheels were used as the means of propulsion

166 FITCH'S STEAMBOAT 1787

This remarkable boat appeared on the Delaware River in Pennsylvania. The high frames on each side supported six oars. A steam engine drove a crank rod which worked the oars alternately

167 MILLER AND SYMINGTON'S TWIN-HULLED STEAMBOAT 1788

The engine was fitted in one hull and the boiler in the other. In the centre were two paddle wheels, placed one behind the other. They propelled the boat at 5 knots

AIR

168 MONTGOLFIER HOT-AIR BALLOON 1783
Man's first successful flight was made in this balloon. It was filled with hot air, and two Frenchmen, Pilâtre de Rozier and Marquis d'Arlandes, flew from the centre of Paris for a distance of 5 miles. The balloon was made by the Montgolfier Brothers

169 HYDROGEN-FILLED BALLOON 1785
Hydrogen gas was used to fill the balloon and a longer flight was now possible. A Professor Charles was able to reach a height of 10,000 feet and also to demonstrate landing and take-off

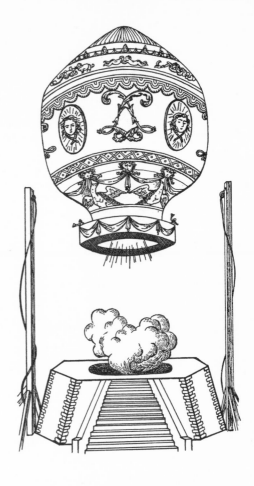

170 LUNARDI'S BALLOON 1784
This balloon was flown in London by the Italian, Lunardi. It was filled with hydrogen and fitted with oars which he hoped would help him to control the balloon. The experiment was not very successful, but Lunardi continued to look for a method of steering balloons

171 MEUNIER'S AIRSHIP DESIGN 1785
This machine never left the planning stage, but Meunier pointed out it would need to be elongated and require great power to drive it through the air. His ideas were put into practice in the nineteenth century

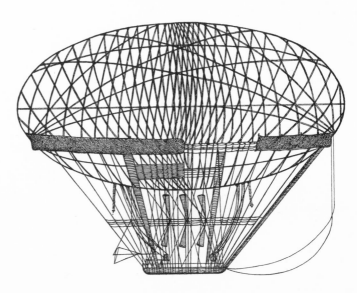

The 19th Century
LAND

172 BREAKING STONES FOR ROADBUILDING
Telford's roads in the early nineteenth century needed stones of a certain size and weight for particular road layers, and masons were kept hard at work providing a steady supply

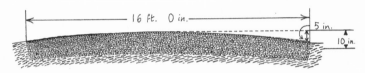

173 MACADAM ROAD SECTION *c.* 1816
John MacAdam was a Scotsman who worked on roads in the West of England before being put in charge of roads throughout Britain. He rejected Telford's deep foundations, concentrating instead on a gravel surface ground smooth by the continuous action of coach and waggon wheels. After 1830 road rollers came into use and British roads were in better condition than they had been at any time since the Romans were in the country

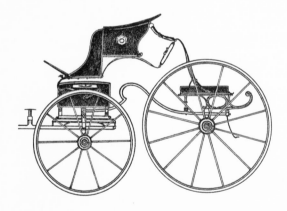

174 PHAETON *c.* 1802
Various styles of this vehicle had existed for over 100 years. This particular model was perched high on elaborate springing

175 CHARIOT *c.* 1809
A four-wheeled carriage mounted on elliptical springs. The boot is situated at the front beneath a high driving seat

176 A GIG 1815
The nineteenth century equivalent of a modern sports car. This open two-wheeled cart was built for one person

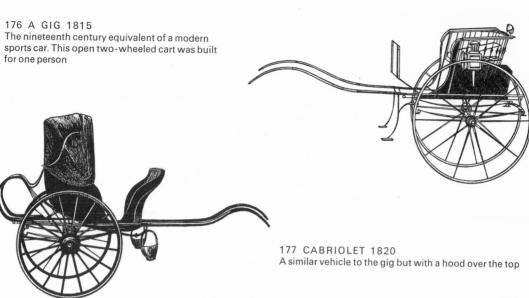

177 CABRIOLET 1820
A similar vehicle to the gig but with a hood over the top

178 BAROUCHE 1830
An elegant four-wheeled carriage with a hood which came up to the half-way position only. It was sometimes called a half-headed carriage

179 STAGE COACH c. 1830
Stage coach services covered most parts of the British Isles, the Continent, and the United States. The British type above carried passengers both inside and outside, and was drawn by teams of horses changed at regular intervals. They made excellent time on the new MacAdam roads, but were undermined by cheap rail travel by the mid-century

180 MAIL COACH *c.* 1835

The mail coach services extended to many parts of Britain after 1784. The swift and safe despatch of mail was guaranteed. These vehicles were faster than the ordinary stagecoaches, and travel for passengers was more expensive

181 BROUGHAM 1840

Introduced by Lord Brougham in the 1830s. It was a compact closed carriage which was drawn by one horse. The cab was mounted on elliptical springs

182 LANDAU 1850

This vehicle was owned by the very wealthy and still survives today for ceremonial purposes. It possessed the distinct advantage of a three-in-one carriage. It could be used as a completely closed carriage, or as a barouche with the half hood, or as an open carriage

183 BUGGY 1860

In the United States, European styles were widely copied, but in the 1850s a distinctive type of vehicle made its appearance. Its chief characteristic was the light construction. Four high wheels and a thin frame supported the carriage and canopy

184 VICTORIA *c.* 1870
A carriage used by the well-to-do in Britain and the United States. It was used essentially as a park carriage

185 HANSOM CAB *c.* 1870
Designed by Joseph Hansom and patented in 1834. London streets were full of these vehicles which could be hired. They were somewhat unstable with two high wheels and pulled by one horse. The driver sat high up on a dicky seat at the rear and received instructions through a trap door in the roof

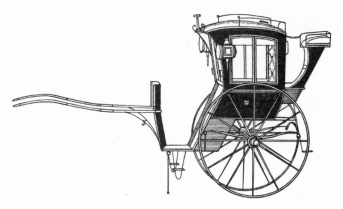

186 SURREY *c.* 1880
A canopy-top surrey, or 'Surrey with a fringe on top'. This specifically American vehicle had curtains, a storm apron, and lamps. It was a four seater family carriage

187 TOWN AND COUNTRY CARRIAGE
c. 1880
This high-set well sprung vehicle was extremely comfortable and was very suitable for long distance travel as well as for town use

188 GURNEY'S STEAM CARRIAGE 1827

In 1826, Sir Goldsworthy Gurney produced a reliable boiler which ran on a mixture of coke and charcoal. An efficient two-cylinder engine was built which developed 12 horse-power. The picture shows a two-ton Gurney steam carriage used on the London to Bath run

189 HANCOCK'S 'ENTERPRISE' 1833

A fourteen seater steam coach invented by Walter Hancock. His improved boilers using engine-driven fans were fitted to steam coaches which were used on services in the London area

190 CHURCH'S STEAM CARRIAGE 1835

An elaborately decorated three-wheeled steam coach invented by Doctor Church, and used on a route from London to Birmingham

191 THE 'AUTOMATON' 1836

Another of Hancock's steam coaches. In spite of the possibilities of this new form of transport, public hostility and the development of the railways prevented the creation of a nation-wide network

192 SHILLIBEER'S OMNIBUS 1829
George Shillibeer was a coach builder in Paris, and there he saw light short-haul omnibuses in use. He went to live in London, and built two 22-seater three-horse buses which began regular timetabled services in the city in 1829

193 TILLING 'KNIFEBOARD' OMNIBUS 1851
Thomas Tilling's company was a well-known private firm in London which ran the first buses to carry passengers on the roof. All told, 24 passengers were carried, those on the top deck sitting back to back on a long bench nicknamed the 'knifeboard'

194 LONDON GENERAL OMNIBUS COMPANY BUS 1856
The London General Omnibus Company competed with private companies like Tillings, and also with a French-owned company, for passengers in London. They used the standard type of vehicle with knifeboard seating on the upper deck

195 DE TIVOLI'S PATENT OMNIBUS 1860
Another knifeboard omnibus introduced on to the London streets in the second half of the nineteenth century

63

196 G. F. TRAIN'S SINGLE DECKER TRAM 1861
Designed by the American G.F. Train, this single decker horse-drawn tram was run on one of
three experimental tracks laid in London in 1861

197 SAN FRANCISCO CABLE CAR 1873
An ideal form of transportation in a city built on steep gradients. This cable car used a system
devised by Andrew Hallidie. The cable ran underground in a slot between the tram rails. The
endless rope wound round pulleys driven by steam power and hauled the cars along

198 BRISTOL HORSE TRAM 1875
The first horse-drawn tram to run in Bristol was of the knifeboard type, having a staircase at
front and rear, and a guard rail on the upper deck

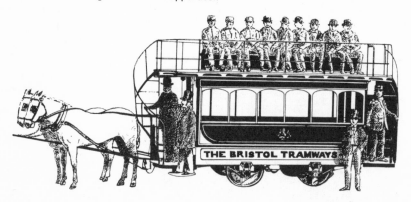

199 BATTERY ELECTRIC TRAMCAR 1883
An Austrian, Anthony Reckenzaum, worked in Britain on a battery driven tramcar. He ran one at Kew in 1883, using accumulators, but as more electric current became available there ceased to be any need for batteries

200 ISLE OF MAN TRAM 1883
A horse-drawn tram used in Douglas, Isle of Man. Closed staircases are situated at each end, and the guard rail on the upper deck is enclosed

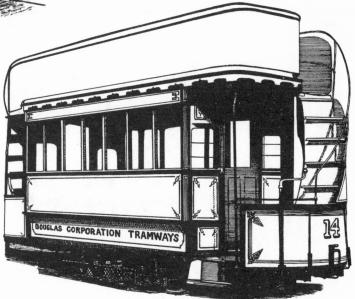

201 NEW YORK OMNIBUS 1880
This New York bus was highly painted and elaborately decorated. Entrance for passengers was through a door at the rear

202 HORSE OMNIBUS 1895
In the 1880s, the London Road Car Company introduced horse-drawn omnibuses with a stairway at the rear and with 'garden' seats placed across the vehicle. These replaced the knifeboard down the centre

203 STEAM TRAM 1890
Trams driven by steam were used in America, Europe, and Australia, but in general there was a good deal of public hostility because of the noise and smoke which filled the city streets. It was found practicable to use separate locomotives drawing a trailer car

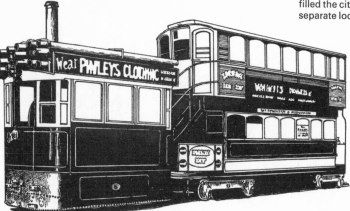

204 BRITISH ELECTRIC TRAM 1895
The overhead trolley and trolley pole were invented in the USA in the 1880s. Britain's first electric tram appeared in Leeds in 1891

205 DE DION TWELVE SEATER BUS 1898
A twelve-seater steam-driven bus introduced in Paris at the end of the nineteenth century

206 DRAISIENNE (HOBBY-HORSE) 1818
A simple vehicle consisting of a crossbar and two wheels. The rider sat astride and propelled himself along with his feet against the ground. It made its appearance in Paris in 1816, and in London in 1818 where it was called the 'dandy-horse'

207 MACMILLAN'S BICYCLE 1839
A Scot, Kirkpatrick MacMillan, improved the dandy-horse by adding cranks, pedals, and driving rods which turned the rear wheel. This was the first real bicycle

208 VELOCIPEDE BICYCLE (BONESHAKER) 1867
In 1865, two Frenchmen, Lallement and Michaux, made the first bicycle with rotary cranks which were fitted to the axle of the front wheel. The machines were very popular, but were heavy and vibrated considerably

209 THE ORDINARY (PENNY FARTHING) BICYCLE c. 1872
Lighter metal wheels were developed with solid rubber tyres attached. To gain more speed, front wheels became larger while the rear wheel shrank in size. The rider sat high over the front wheel

210 STARLEY'S SAFETY BICYCLE 1885
Invented by H. J. Lawson in 1876, but appeared in a practical form as James Starley's Rover bicycle in 1885. It was a low bicycle and was chain driven. In 1888 Dunানlop's pneumatic tyre set the seal on the popularity of the bicycle

211 BENZ THREE-WHEELER CAR 1888
Siegfried Markus, an Austrian, produced a four-wheeled carriage in 1875 driven by an internal combustion engine, but ten years later, Gottlieb Daimler and Carl Benz made similar vehicles which were more successful. Benz' carriages were three-wheelers, with an engine below the seat driving the rear axle by means of chains and a primitive form of clutch

212 DAIMLER 1895
This four-wheeled vehicle was a two-seater with the engine at the rear. It was water cooled and had four gears

213 A LUTZMANN 1895
This model was an elaborate attempt to retain the lines of the carriage. The front wheels were mounted on elliptical springs. The clothes worn by the motorists indicate the rigours of travel in the open cars of the 1890s

214 A DURYEA 1895
In 1893, Charles Duryea built the first petrol-driven American car. His improved models were fast, and competed well with imported European cars

215 JENATZY'S ELECTRIC CAR 1899
Built by Camille Jenatzy, a Belgian, this car was the first to be driven by an electric motor. The bullet-shaped body fitted to a four-wheeled chassis enabled the car to reach a speed of over 60 m.p.h

216 CHIRK AQUEDUCT, NORTH WALES 1801
Telford designed this aqueduct to carry the Ellesmere Canal across the River Ceiriog. In all there were ten arches which linked solid stone piers. Beyond the aqueduct lies a tunnel which takes the canal through a nearby hillside

217 LOCKS ON THE SEVERN CANAL
Locks were in use in many countries to carry canals over rising ground. The picture shows a barge entering a lock prior to being raised on to the next level. It is drawn by a steam tug which began to replace horses towards the end of the nineteenth century

218 PONT-Y-CYSYLLTE AQUEDUCT, NORTH WALES 1805
Another superb example of Telford's work on the Ellesmere Canal. In this instance the canal crossed the River Dee. Cast iron troughs were laid across stone piers, making a total length of 1000 feet

219 BARGE 1830
The type of barge used in Britain on the Grand Trunk Canal. It was 70 feet long and 7½ feet wide

220 OPENING OF THE SUEZ CANAL 1869
The ship canal, for cutting short long sea journeys, was used on an increasing scale as the century progressed. Ferdinand de Lesseps planned the Suez Canal to join the Mediterranean to the Red Sea, and it was opened in 1869. The sea route to India was considerably shortened, and this favoured the steamer because sailing ships were unable to use the Canal

221 SURREY IRON RAILWAY 1801
The iron track railway came into its own with the opening of the Surrey Iron Railway in South London. It was built over a distance of nine miles from Wandsworth to Croydon. The trucks were horse-drawn, and only goods were carried

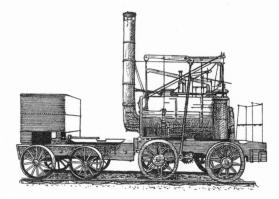

222 'PUFFING BILLY' 1813
Built by William Hedley, an engineer at Wylam Colliery near Newcastle. It was used to haul coal trucks from the pithead to the River Tyne. Two cylinders, working alternately, were fitted, and the axles were coupled by cogwheels

223 TREVITHICK'S LOCOMOTIVE 1804
Richard Trevithick is usually regarded as the 'Father of the Locomotive' He ran this locomotive on rails at Pen-y-darran iron works in South Wales, and it was the first one designed for rail transport. A large flywheel and cogwheel connected the front and rear axles. The locomotive pulled goods and passengers at five m.p.h.

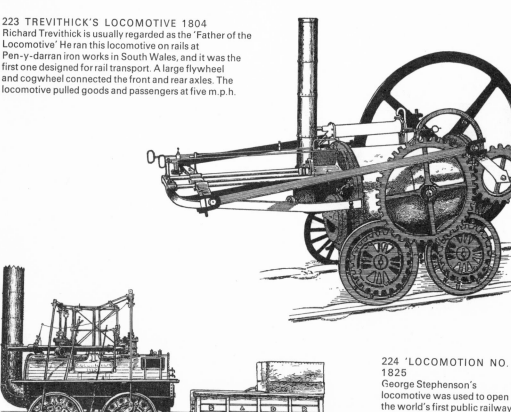

224 'LOCOMOTION NO. I' 1825
George Stephenson's locomotive was used to open the world's first public railway from Stockton to Darlington in 1825. It pulled a train of about 90 tons and reached a speed of 12 m.p.h.

225 'ROCKET' 1829

George Stephenson and his son Robert won the £500 prize offered by the Liverpool to Manchester Line for the best locomotive at the Rainhill Trials. 'The Rocket's' cylinders were angled on the original design, but later they were moved to near horizontal for smoother running. The driving wheels were 3 feet 9 inches across and speeds of around 30 m.p.h. were reached

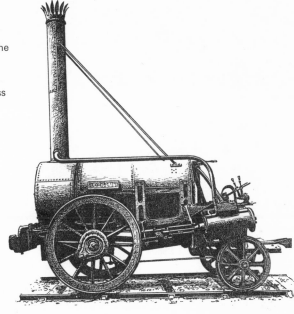

226 AMERICAN LOCOMOTIVE 1831

The first locomotive used in the USA was the 'Stourbridge Lion', imported from Britain in 1829. The 'Dewitt Clinton', pictured above, went into service in 1831 on the Mohawk and Hudson Railroad. Two pairs of coupled driving wheels were a notable feature of this locomotive

227 'PLANET' TYPE LOCOMOTIVE 1832

Outside cylinders disappeared with this type of locomotive. Instead they were located between the wheels under the smoke box. Another version of this locomotive had four coupled driving wheels and was used for goods traffic

228 'PATENTEE' TYPE LOCOMOTIVE 1834
The first design to include a 2–2–2 wheel arrangement. An extra pair of trailing wheels supported a bigger boiler and firebox. A steam operated brake was also fitted. Sandwich frame construction was used, that is, wood strengthened by iron plates

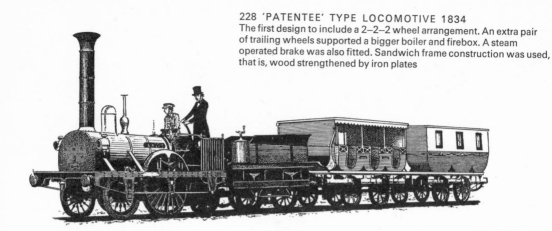

229 'LONG-BOILER' LOCOMOTIVE 1840s
This attempt to produce larger locomotives met with limited success. The engine wheelbase was somewhat short for the long boiler, and the locomotive was very unsteady at high speeds. Inside and outside cylinders were fitted, but neither proved really effective

230 BRITISH LOCOMOTIVE 'LORD OF THE ISLES' 1851
A successful larger type locomotive built by Daniel Gooch for the Great Western Railway. The large driving wheels were 8 feet in diameter, and to take the bigger boiler a wheel arrangement of 4–2–2 was incorporated. One interesting feature is that even by the 1850s British locomotives were not provided with protection for the crew

231 AMERICAN LOCOMOTIVE 1850
American locomotives were now taking on the distinctive appearance which we associate with
countless Western films. The tall chimney and the 'cowcatcher' grid at the front are familiar,
but other features included bogie wheels and better protection for the crew. The four bogie wheels
at the front of the locomotive are swivelled and not arranged as two separate pairs on axles

232 A STIRLING 'SINGLE-WHEELER', BRITISH 1870
Eight feet driving wheels enabled this locomotive to travel at quite high speeds. Swivel bogies
were built in front of the driving wheels, and a slightly more comfortable cab was provided for
.the crew

233 AMERICAN LOCOMOTIVE 1870s
The 4–4–0 wheel arrangement appeared first
in the United States. From 1869 onwards the
Westinghouse compressed-air brake was fitted
to trains, and this allowed higher speeds. The
bell and headlamp were carried as part of the
locomotive's warning system

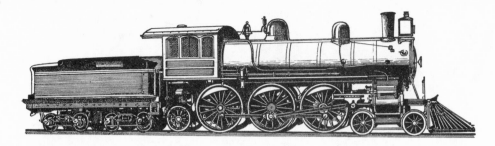

234 AMERICAN 'PACIFIC' LOCOMOTIVE 1889
More powerful locomotives were needed to haul heavy trains for long distances in the USA.
Larger wheelbases were used to carry the huge boilers, and the 4–6–2, or 'Pacific', wheel
arrangement was developed

235 BRITISH 4–4–0 LOCOMOTIVE 1892
A powerful locomotive employed on services from London to the South Coast. The driving wheels
were now smaller, and a more complete cab was included. A high boiler pressure was
obtained for fast working.

236 BRITAIN'S FIRST 4–6–0 LOCOMOTIVE 1894
This locomotive was built for the Highland Railway, and included in its design was a large
boiler, and a bigger firebox with wider grate. The driving wheels were medium sized

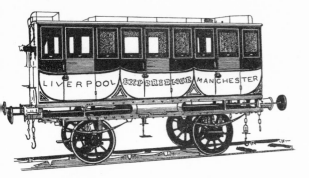

237 CARRIAGE OF THE LIVERPOOL TO MANCHESTER RAILWAY 1834
A first class carriage mounted on four wheels and still showing signs of the old stage coach design used for carriages on the earliest railways. The carriage is divided into three compartments, with seating for six passengers in each. Windows are fitted in the doors and also alongside the seats

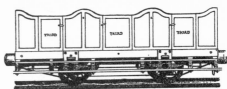

238 THIRD CLASS OPEN CARRIAGE 1840
Cheap third class travel was introduced by the end of the 1830s. No effort was made to provide comfort for third class passengers. Seats were wooden, and the carriage was completely open to the elements

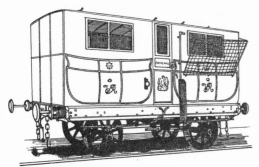

239 TRAVELLING POST OFFICE 1840
This special carriage was first used on the Grand Junction Railway between Birmingham and Warrington in 1838. Letters were sorted in the carriage ready for delivery, and a net was constructed on the side to pick up mail bags so that the train did not have to stop

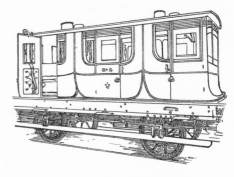

240 BED CARRIAGE 1842
A specially built carriage made by the London to Birmingham Railway for Queen Adelaide in 1842. The seat in the centre compartment could be reclined for sleeping

242 THIRD CLASS COACH 1854
Since 1844, third class travel had been fixed at one penny per mile, and as companies were forced to run third class trains, some effort was made to provide more comfort. The carriages were now covered, but the inside was sparsely furnished, and there were no compartment divisions

241 FIRST CLASS COACH 1854
A three compartment coach. Furnishings consisted of plush upholstery, head rests and arm rests, and leather straps on the windows

243 SANKEY VIADUCT 1829
The viaduct was designed by George Stephenson to carry the Liverpool to Manchester Railway across Sankey Brook. Nine large stone arches were used in its construction

244 HIGH LEVEL VIADUCT, NEWCASTLE 1849
Robert Stephenson's bridge over the Tyne was built across five stone piers. It was built on two levels, with the railway line on top and a road deck below

245 BRITANNIA TUBULAR BRIDGE, WALES 1850
Built by Robert Stephenson across the Menai Straits. Three stone piers support tubular girders made from wrought iron plates, and form two 460 foot spans. Trains cross into Anglesey from the Welsh mainland over the bridge

246 ROYAL ALBERT BRIDGE, SALTASH 1859
Completed by Isambard Brunel, in the year of his death, to carry the Great Western Railway across
the River Tamar into Cornwall. Two iron arches are connected to three stone piers to carry the
single-track line

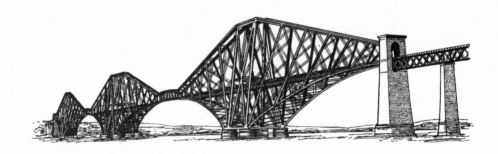

247 FORTH BRIDGE, SCOTLAND 1890
A cantilever structure built by Fowler and Baker across
the Forth. This railway bridge has two spans, each 1710
feet long, and three cantilevers joined by girder spans

248 NEW YORK OVERHEAD RAILWAY *c.* 1870
Some American cities favoured overhead railways rather
than, or as well as, underground systems, These lines
were built on trestles over the city streets. They were
cheaper to run than the Subway, and were used in
New York from 1870 onwards. Until the twentieth century
the locomotives were steam-driven, and they were
usually of the tank engine type as shown above

**249 BAKER STREET
UNDERGROUND STATION
1863**
The Metropolitan Railway in London
was the world's first underground
steam railway. The line ran in trenches
below street level, and the trenches
were roofed

**250 ELECTRIC TUBE AND LOCOMOTIVE
1890**
The world's first electric tube railway was the City
and South London line opened in 1890. Steel tube
tunnels carried the running track and current rails.
It was impossible to use steam locomotives in the
confined atmosphere of the tubes, so the carriages
were hauled by electric locomotives

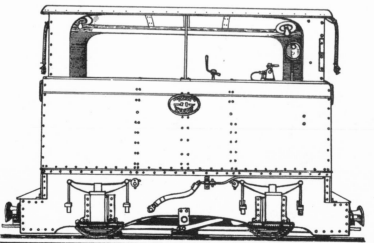

WATER

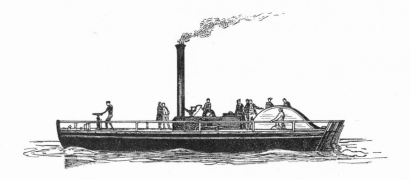

251 THE *CHARLOTTE DUNDAS* 1802
Designed by William Symington, and tried out on
the Forth-Clyde Canal. She was the first practical
steamboat. A stern paddle wheel was placed between
twin rudders, enabling her to tow two 70 ton
barges on her trials

252 THE *CLERMONT* 1807
The ship was the first steamer to carry passengers
on a commercial service. Robert Fulton designed
her to run on the Hudson River between New York
and Albany. A Boulton and Watt engine powered the
ship, which was 130 feet long, by means of paddle
wheels placed either side of the hull

253 THE *COMET* 1812
Henry Bell ran this ship on the Clyde to open Europe's
first steamer service in 1812. She was propelled by a
four horse-power engine, and this power was
supplemented by a sail. The funnel was also used as
a mast

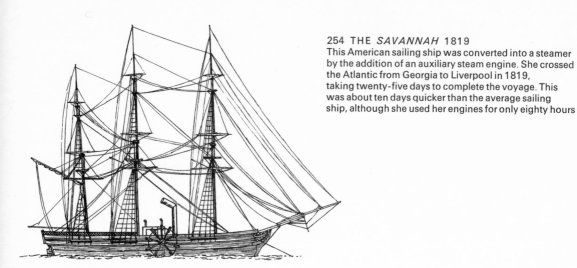

254 THE *SAVANNAH* 1819
This American sailing ship was converted into a steamer by the addition of an auxiliary steam engine. She crossed the Atlantic from Georgia to Liverpool in 1819, taking twenty-five days to complete the voyage. This was about ten days quicker than the average sailing ship, although she used her engines for only eighty hours

255 THE *CURAÇAO* 1826
A wooden paddler, built at Dover for the Dutch Navy, which crossed the Atlantic from Rotterdam to the West Indies in one month using steam only. She made regular crossings between 1826 and 1830

256 THE *SIRIUS* 1838
An American hired this Irish packet boat to cross to New York in 1838. She completed the voyage in nineteen days, but not before all the fuel had been consumed, and a good deal of the ship's furniture also

257 BRUNEL'S *GREAT WESTERN* 1838
Isambard Brunel built this ship to carry passengers from Bristol to New York. She reached
New York immediately after the *Sirius,* and completely eclipsed that ship's arrival, having taken
only fifteen days for the voyage. She was 276 feet long, and weighed 1320 tons

258 A PADDLE STEAMER 1838
Engineers did not yet have the fullest confidence
in their engines. Paddle wheels were liable to
break, so masts with full sail were incorporated
in ship designs; just in case

259 THE *ARCHIMEDES* 1839
One of the first screw-driven vessels.
This form of propulsion was a better
alternative to paddle wheels because
the propellers operated in the calmer
waters at the stern of the ship
(figure 260). The *Archimedes*
reached up to 13 knots

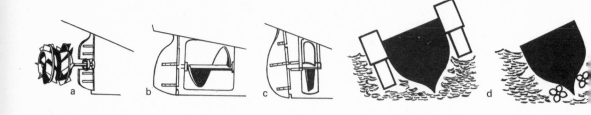

260 SCREW PROPELLER DIAGRAMS 1836–9
(a) John Ericsson's double propeller, 1836, (b) Smith's screw, 1836, (c) Ericsson's improved propeller, 1839, (d) The advantage of screw propulsion over paddles

261 THE *BRITANNIA* 1840
When regular Atlantic services were started in 1840 by Samuel Cunard, the sailing ship was doomed. Cunard's *Britannia* was one of the ships used, and she carried mail as well as passengers

262 THE *HINDOOSTAN* 1842
Sailing ships still dominated the route to the Far East, but, since 1825, steamships had been making voyages to India. In the 1840s, the Peninsular and Orient Line put into service a two-funnelled steamer with side paddles

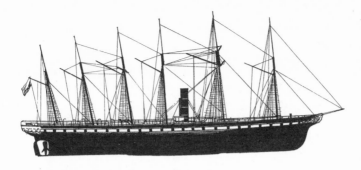

263 THE *GREAT BRITAIN* 1843
Brunel decided that this ship should be driven by screw propellers. He also designed her to be
built of iron instead of wood. She weighed 3,000 tons and was well over 300 feet long,
and in 1845 she crossed the Atlantic in $14\frac{1}{2}$ days

264 THE *GREAT EASTERN* 1858
An ill-fated ship which was far in advance of her time. No larger ship was built until the early
1900s. In this design, Brunel incorporated paddle wheels, a huge propeller, two sets of engines,
five funnels, and six masts with full sail. She was commercially unsuccessful, and in 1866 she was
employed to lay a telegraph cable across the Atlantic. She ended her life as a floating fair

265 THE *OCEANIC* 1871
Built for the White Star Line, this vessel was the first of the modern fast luxury liners. She ran
between New York and Liverpool, and was a great success. Nearly 4,000 tons in weight, the ship
was rigged as a four-master, and her single-screw engines gave a speed of nearly 15 knots

266 A MISSISSIPPI STEAMER *c.* 1870
These unique paddle steamers were a common sight on the Mississippi, operating down to New Orleans. The single paddle wheel was situated either towards, or at, the stern, and was made up of blades extending right across the boat

267 THE *BOTHNIA* 1874
This vessel was built of iron and was fitted with compound engines which drove screw propellers. Sails were still carried, but the new engines were very efficient and used far less fuel than earlier versions. This was a great step forward because more space could be allocated to passengers and cargo

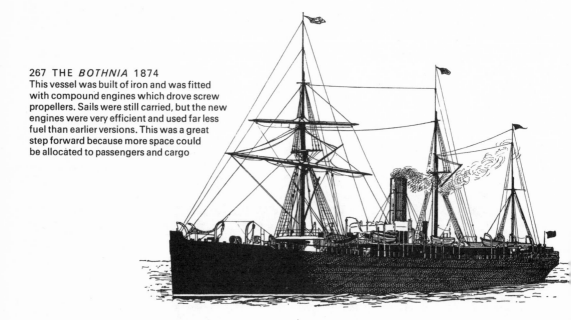

268 THE *TURBINIA* 1897
The steam turbine engine was very efficient, largely because steel had replaced iron as an everyday material. Charles Parsons applied his new engine to a small 44 ton launch, the *Turbinia,* in 1897, and reached the fantastic speed of 35 knots

269 EAST INDIAMAN 1817
One of the last of the East India Company's old style
sailing ships, soon to be replaced by the Blackwall
frigates (diagram 271). The vessel above, the
Thomas Coutts, set up a sailing ship record for the
voyage from England to China in 1826. The sailing ship
continued on the run to the East for many years, although
the first steamer had reached India in 1825

270 A SLOOP 1826
A fast naval ship with flush decks.
A spritsail and driver were fitted in
addition to the sails on the other masts

271 A BLACKWALL FRIGATE 1837
A speedier and more efficient ship was
needed to replace the large East Indiamen,
and the Blackwall Frigate was designed
to these requirements. Although they
were heavy vessels, they were less
cumbersome than their predecessors,
and they handled well

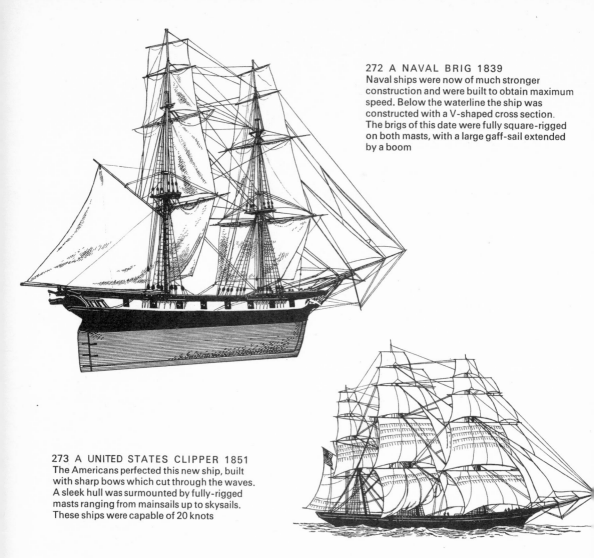

272 A NAVAL BRIG 1839
Naval ships were now of much stronger
construction and were built to obtain maximum
speed. Below the waterline the ship was
constructed with a V-shaped cross section.
The brigs of this date were fully square-rigged
on both masts, with a large gaff-sail extended
by a boom

273 A UNITED STATES CLIPPER 1851
The Americans perfected this new ship, built
with sharp bows which cut through the waves.
A sleek hull was surmounted by fully-rigged
masts ranging from mainsails up to skysails.
These ships were capable of 20 knots

274 THE *TAEPING* 1860s
British builders copied the American
designs and eventually supplanted them
on the Eastern run. In 1866, the *Taeping,
Ariel,* and *Serica* all docked in London
within an hour of each other after 99 days
at sea out of Foochow

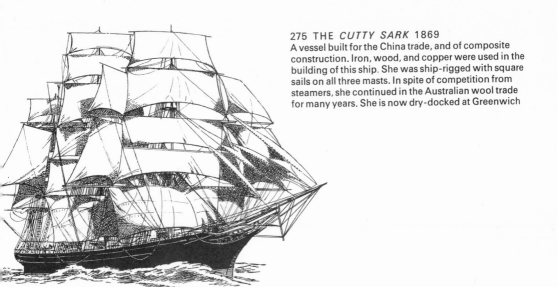

275 THE *CUTTY SARK* 1869
A vessel built for the China trade, and of composite construction. Iron, wood, and copper were used in the building of this ship. She was ship-rigged with square sails on all three masts. In spite of competition from steamers, she continued in the Australian wool trade for many years. She is now dry-docked at Greenwich

276 THE *JOHN OF GAUNT* 1869
An iron clipper ship built at Birkenhead in 1869. She was rigged in the same style as the *Cutty Sark*, and she traded between London and India

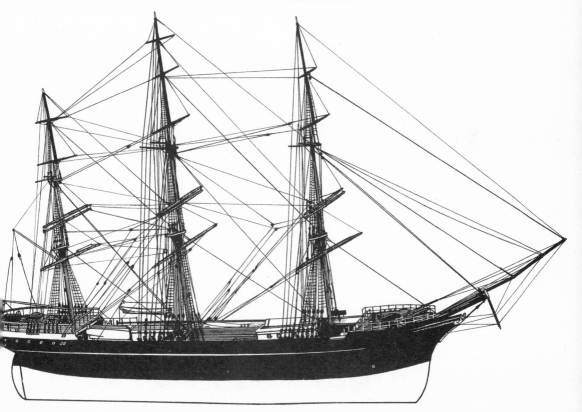

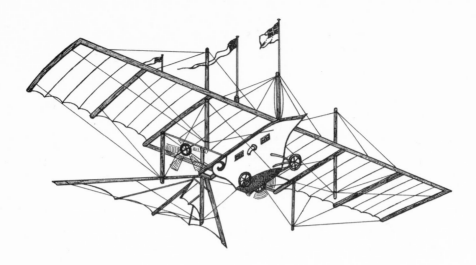

277 HENSON'S AERIAL STEAM CARRIAGE 1847

William Henson was an Englishman who based his work on the ideas put forward by Sir George Cayley. With John Stringfellow, he designed and built the above model, driven by a light steam engine. However, trials in 1847 failed, and he gave up the work

278 CAYLEY'S GLIDER 1849

One of several models made by Sir George Cayley in the first half of the nineteenth century, based on his study of aerodynamics. In particular he saw that if a machine with wings was forced forward, it would create air resistance under the wings and gain the necessary lift to take to the air. However, the power to drive it forward was the problem, because the steam engine was not really suited to flying machines.

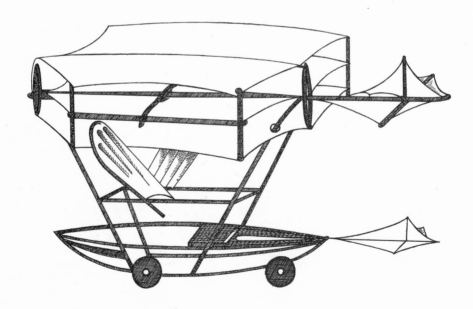

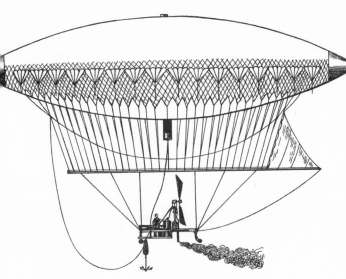

279 GIFFARD'S STEAM DRIVEN AIRSHIP 1852
The first powered flight was made by Henri Giffard, a Frenchman. This took place in 1852 in a cigar-shaped airship fitted with a light steam engine. He flew successfully at about five miles an hour, but he realised that his 130 foot airship was not large enough, and that the steam engine was not the complete answer to the problem of power

280 DU TEMPLE'S AIRCRAFT 1874
A monoplane with tapered wings. The trailing edges were made flexible, a forerunner of modern ailerons. A rudder was fitted at the rear. The engine was designed to drive a screw which measured four metres across, and some authorities state that the machine flew and alighted without damage

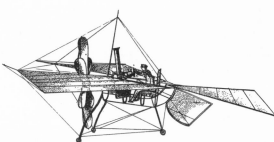

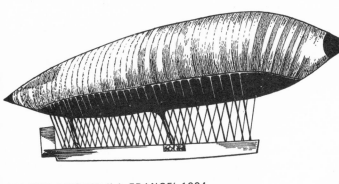

281 THE AIRSHIP 'LA FRANCE' 1884
This *dirigible,* or steerable airship, was driven by battery electric motors. The gas-filled machine was 160 feet long, and was steered by a rudder and driven along by a screw propeller. It was flown by Captains Renard and Krebs

282 LILLIENTHAL'S GLIDER 1895
Otto Lillienthal, a German, made many flights in his gliders, operating them with his legs which he allowed to hang below the machines. He was unfortunately killed in 1896 when on the verge of powered flight

The 20th Century
LAND

283 A FIAT CAR 1900
The Italian Fiat Company was founded in 1899 at Turin. Production of smaller cars was started at the beginning of the twentieth century, and the model above was the first type to be built. It was a typical half-hood car of the period, with the front completely open to the elements

284 A MERCEDES 1901
For its time, this car was well advanced. It was driven by a four-cylinder engine driving the rear wheels by means of a large chain. It was a fast robust car, and very easy to handle. The car was named after a girl called Mercedes Jellinek. The company joined with the Benz Organisation in 1926

285 ROLLS-ROYCE 'SILVER GHOST' 1907
This luxurious car was designed by Henry Royce specifically as a motor car, and not an adapted horse carriage. Charles Rolls advised Royce to concentrate on this type of expensive model, and they built their famous works at Derby. Cars of the highest class were produced. They were elegant, noiseless, and completely reliable. The 'Silver Ghost' was driven by a huge six-cylinder engine developing 50 h.p.

286 FORD MODEL T 1909
Motoring was a hobby for the rich until Henry Ford introduced his 'Model T', or 'Tin Lizzie', produced by mass-production methods at Detroit. The car was cheap to buy and economical to run, but it was open at the front and had no doors. Ford said, when he launched the car, 'Any customer can have a car painted any colour he wants, so long as it is black'

287 A LONDON TAXI 1908
The 'Unic' taxi-cab was designed by George Richards. The driver's seat was open, protected only by a projecting roof, while the passengers sat in a covered cab at the rear

288 A CADILLAC 1914
A typical car of this time with square contours. This American Cadillac shows that car builders were now thinking of more integrated designs, with mudguards and wings shaped as part of the car. The company introduced the first electric starter in 1911

289 A MORRIS 1920
Cheap motoring was introduced into Britain by William Morris of Oxford. His first cars were made in 1913, but it was after the war that his 'Bullnosed' Morris made its real impact. The car was driven by a 12 h.p. engine

290 AN AUSTIN SEVEN 1922
This small family car was designed by Herbert Austin in Birmingham, and was one of the most successful cars in the years between the two World Wars

291 MODEL T 1927
The last of fifteen million Model T Fords was sold in
1927. Ford decided that more elegant models were now
necessary. The last Tin Lizzies were completely covered
and were fitted with doors

292 RILEY NINE 1927
The Riley Nine of the late Twenties was an extremely
popular car on the sporting field as well as on the road,
because it was light and fast. It remained virtually
unchanged for ten years

293 A CADILLAC 1936
This American company concentrated on large
expensive cars. The 1936 model came out
at a time when streamlining was popular.
The huge V8, V12, and V16 engines gave the
bonnet an elongated look. The wings were
faired in to the body and running boards had
disappeared. Overdrive, freewheel drive, and
synchromesh gears all appeared in the
United States in the early Thirties

294 A VAUXHALL 1938
This British company was taken over by
General Motors of America in 1926.
The model above, which appeared in 1938,
was the first British mass-produced car to
have an integral body and chassis

295 A MORRIS MINOR 1948

One of the first British designs to come onto the roads after World War II. This Morris Minor, later the Morris 1000, has a compact, rounded appearance and is designed for cheap family motoring. It is still in production at the present time

296 A VOLKSWAGEN 1954

The most successful car ever produced. The 'Beetle' appeared before World War II, and has continued in production with various modifications to the present day. The engine is situated at the rear and is air cooled. The sloping front contains the luggage boot

297 A MERCEDES SPORTS CAR 1954

This is a typical example of a sports model of the 1950s. Sleek low lines with wings streamlined into the body give the appearance of speed and power. The car could be purchased as a roadster with a movable hood, or as a coupé, above, with fixed hood. It was capable of speeds well in excess of 100 m.p.h.

298 CITROEN DS19 1955

A revolutionary French design which is still in production. Of unusual appearance, with the cab set well back and large window areas. The windscreen is of the 'wrap-around' type, and the car's suspension can be adjusted to suit road conditions

299 A FIAT 500 1957

The Italian company has cornered a large share of the small car market with this model. It is a blunt car with no frontal intake and is driven by a rear mounted engine. This two-door economical saloon has a fabric roof, very suitable for warmer climates

300 A 'MINI' CAR 1959

Designed for the British Motor Corporation by Alec Issigonis, this car has proved a sensation. It is compact but has a good turn of speed. Unusual features for the time include a transverse engine that is mounted across the car, front wheel drive, and a common oil sump for engine and gearbox

301 FORD THUNDERBIRD 1960

A typical large, flamboyant model much favoured in the United States. Every comfort is provided for the motorist, with radio, electrically operated retractable roof, powerful engine, and luxurious suspension. The rear bodywork is curved upwards into fins, and bumpers wrap around at front and rear

302 A LOTUS CORTINA 1967

For the specialist motorist the Ford Company of Great Britain has combined with the Lotus Car Company to produce a fast stylish car out of the popular medium range family saloon

303 A ROLLS-ROYCE 1968

Although the Rolls-Royce Company has continued to produce expensive limousines, they have also built sleeker more compact cars, but keeping the distinctive Rolls-Royce radiator grill

304 AN AMPHICAR 1968

An experimental car which aims to combine the attributes of a land vehicle and a boat. Obviously has great possibilities in certain parts of the world where land communication is not highly developed

305 TRIUMPH MOTOR CYCLE 1914

Although the first motor cycles were built in Germany in the 1880s, they did not become popular until the early twentieth century. The Triumph Junior, above, was fitted with an engine placed in the centre of the frame, driving the rear wheel by means of a chain, and developing $2\frac{1}{2}$ h.p.

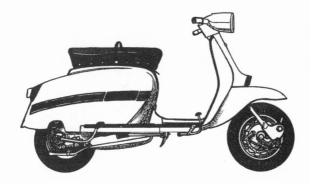

306 A LAMBRETTA SCOOTER 1968

The small motorised scooter has become extremely popular on the Continent of Europe, especially in Italy. Small wheels are covered by mudguards and bodywork to give the rider and pillion maximum protection. The compact engine gives quite high speeds

307 A JAPANESE HONDA MOTOR CYCLE 1969

The Japanese have entered this market, which was dominated by European companies, and have produced very successful machines. The latest models are very powerful and are fitted with every modern gadget including telescopic forks for excellent suspension

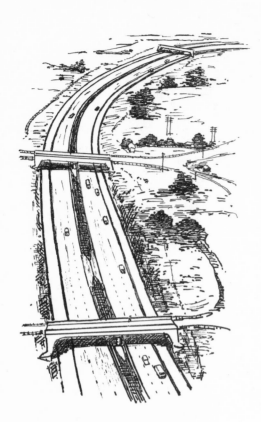

308 MOTORWAY M1 1959
Britain was well behind other countries in constructing a system of motorways. The first, the M1, running from London towards the Midlands, was opened in 1959. Three lanes are provided in each carriageway to allow maximum traffic flow, while road junctions are filtered to avoid the 'T' junction found on ordinary roads. Other roads cross either above or below the motorway

309 SAN BERNADINO FREEWAY USA 1960s
An American motorway in California showing a 'cloverleaf' junction which allows traffic to filter from the minor road on to the freeway. The rule of the road in the USA is keep to the right

310 RUSH HOUR TRAFFIC 1960s
This is a typical scene at certain times of the day in most modern cities. The combination of public, commercial and private transport clogs the city streets and causes delays, sometimes of several hours

311 A LORRY 1930s
By the Thirties goods vehicles were becoming larger and more powerful, and were a threat to the railways. This Guy lorry is typical of the time and was fitted with a diesel engine

312 A MECHANICAL HORSE 1950s
A three-wheeled, short haul vehicle fitted with a swivel trailer. It has proved most useful in city streets for loading and delivery because of its very tight turning circle

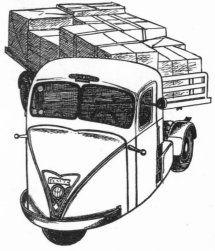

313 A 'UNIC' 10-TON LORRY 1969
A French vehicle driven by a diesel engine and used for carrying such loads as bricks or sand. The truck section of the lorry will tip backwards or to the side, whichever is required, and the driver is provided with good all-round vision

314 AN ARTICULATED LORRY 1969
Lorries like the Italian model below have now become so long that they have to be fitted with articulated trailers to make turning simpler. Huge loads can be transported in these vehicles, which are capable of great speeds, especially along the Autostrada in Italy

315 A LISBON TRAM 1900

A single decker tram using clerestory windows in the roof. The trolley pole transmits power from overhead wires. This type of tram is now used for carrying tourists about the city

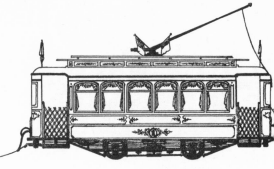

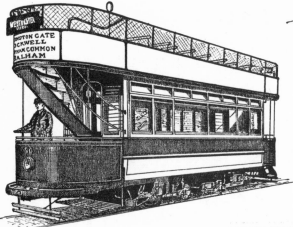

316 LONDON COUNTY COUNCIL ELECTRIC TRAM 1903

The electric tram proved a better alternative to the steam tram. It was cheaper to run, smokeless, and less noisy. Roofless double-deckers were still considered safer than covered trams at this time.

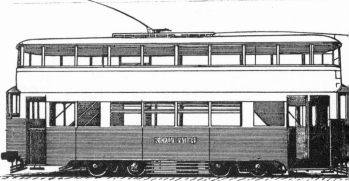

317 A FELTHAM TRAM 1920s

Following World War I, the London County Council ordered new trams which were fast and comfortable. The new Feltham class provided ample room for passengers, even during the rush hour. The stairways and upper deck were completely enclosed

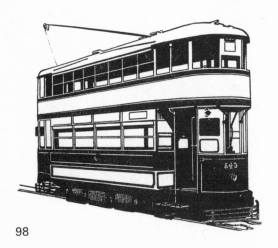

318 A BIRMINGHAM TRAM 1930

This square style tram was built for Birmingham Corporation in 1930. It was completely enclosed, and remained in service until 1953 when the city's trams were withdrawn

319 SAN FRANCISCO CABLE CAR 1940s
For about one hundred years, the cable car system has operated in San Francisco (figure 197). Today they still run on the hilly city streets, and they are a great tourist attraction

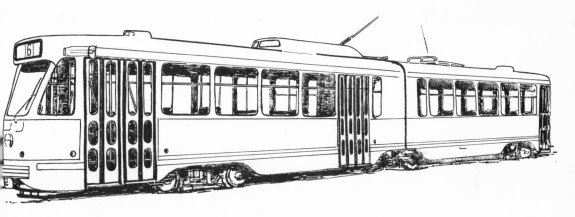

320 A BRUSSELS ARTICULATED TRAM 1950s
Single decker trams have proved popular on the Continent, where trams have continued in service far longer than in Britain. Articulated vehicles have been built so that more passengers can be carried. The tram above is built on three bogies, with electrically operated doors at front, centre, and rear

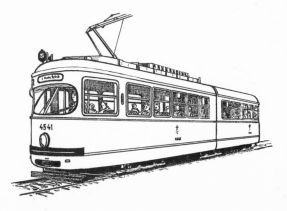

321 A VIENNESE TRAM 1960s
A modern streamlined articulated tramcar in use in the Austrian capital

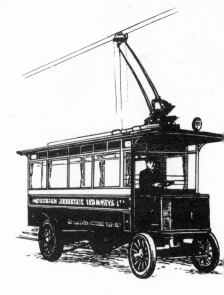

322 'ORION' TYPE MOTOR BUS 1904
One of the earliest motor buses in Britain. The body still resembles that of the horse-drawn bus, the only concession to the motor age being the chassis and engine

323 FIRST TROLLEYBUS IN BRITAIN 1909
The Germans and French produced the first trolleybuses which could run either on or off rails. Swivelling poles were used, and in Britain the idea of twin trolleys was put forward

324 'B' TYPE OMNIBUS 1910
As more motor buses were built, companies tried to produce the best model. The London General made history with the 'B' type of 1910. It was a standardised petrol driven vehicle with a 30 h.p. engine, and it was built to carry 30 passengers

325 'N.S.' TYPE OMNIBUS 1923
London was slow to accept innovations, and even though the new 'N.S.' type had an exceptionally low centre of gravity, no roof was allowed until 1925. Solid tyres were fitted because pneumatic tyres were allowed only on single deckers until 1928

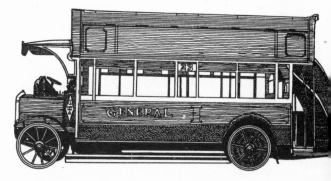

326 DAIMLER-BENZ DOUBLE DECKER OMNIBUS 1926
A roofed and enclosed cab double decker, introduced in the middle Twenties. Staircase at the rear was still open

327 A TROLLEYBUS 1931
A very popular vehicle in Britain, which was used in increasing numbers to replace the tramcar. Since 1945 most of these vehicles have been withdrawn, and only a few towns still run them

328 MIDLAND RED BUS 1932
A comfortable and completely enclosed bus built for the Midland Red Company. Entrance was at the rear, with a closed staircase to the upper deck

329 A LONDON BUS 1939
The last model to go into service before
World War II. It was a stylish streamlined
vehicle with clean lines, and powered by a
diesel engine

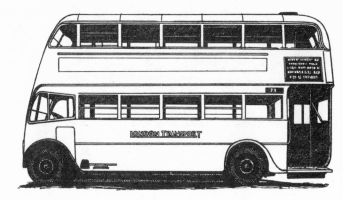

330 A LEYLAND 'ATLANTEAN' 1958
The Leyland Company produced the 78-
seater bus with an electrically operated front
entrance, and staircase just behind the
driver's cab. The engine is located at the rear,
making maintenance much easier

331 MOTORWAY BUS 1960s
High speed motorway buses have made their
appearance in Britain since the opening of the M1
in 1959. They are extremely comfortable, and are
equipped with toilet facilities and luggage space

332 EUROPEAN TOURING COACH 1969
The touring coach, which caters for cheap holiday travel in Europe, is becoming increasingly popular. It is lavishly equipped and fully air conditioned for complete comfort. Transparent roof panels give unobstructed viewing, and independent braking systems make for safety in mountain passes

333 AMERICAN GREYHOUND LONG DISTANCE BUS 1960s
Trans-Continental bus services have been established in the USA as an alternative to rail transport. The Greyhound 'Scenicruiser', having one and a half decks, was first built in the middle fifties. 43 seats are provided along with toilet facilities and air conditioning. Twin diesels power the bus

334 A LONDON 'ROUTEMASTER' 1960s
Almost 30 feet long, this huge bus has seating for 72 passengers. It is remarkably light for its size, and has completely taken the place of the tram in the capital

335 A GREAT WESTERN RAILWAY
LOCOMOTIVE 1903

4–4–0 locomotives carried out the main express work in the
early years of this century. The 'City of Truro' was
built with a conical shaped boiler. In 1904 this
locomotive ran at over 100 m.p.h. on a journey to Plymouth

336 GERMAN P8 LOCOMOTIVE 1908

A 4–6–0 locomotive which was a maid-of-all-work on
German railways in the years up to World War II. They
were equipped with six-foot driving wheels, and were
excellent climbers

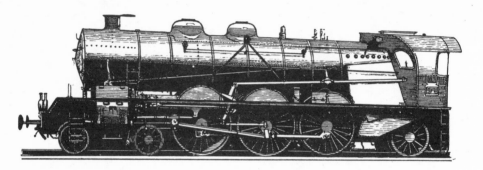

337 A FRENCH LOCOMOTIVE 1912

This Pacific type locomotive was built for the Paris, Lyons, and Mediterranean Railway in 1912.
It was a four-cylinder simple engine, but was later converted to compound working (figure 340)

338 A TANK LOCOMOTIVE 1913

The carrying of water in a tender was the usual practice for express locomotives, but the tank
engine was built for short-haul work. Tanks were either built in 'saddle' style over the boiler,
or in oblong tanks either side of the boiler

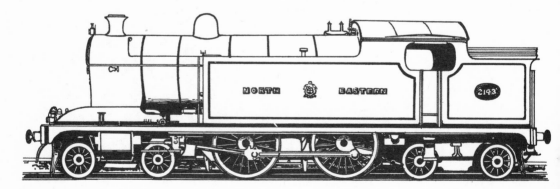

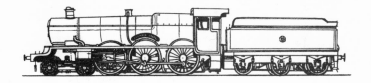

339 A 'CASTLE' CLASS LOCOMOTIVE 1920s
The Great Western Railway turned to the 4–6–0 locomotive to work high speed expresses to the West of England

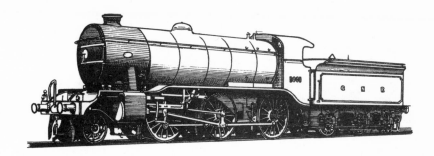

340 A 2–6–0 K3 TYPE LOCOMOTIVE 1920s
Built by Gresley for the Great Northern Railway, prior to the sweeping amalgamations which took place in Britain in 1923. This locomotive was intended for mixed traffic working, and was built with six driving wheels and two leading bogies

341 A COMPOUND LOCOMOTIVE 1920s
The compound locomotive was used successfully in the 1880s, and in 1904 further models were ordered for the Midland Railway. On the compound locomotive, one high pressure cylinder inside the frame passed steam on to two low pressure cylinders outside. These models were highly successful and were improved in the 1920s

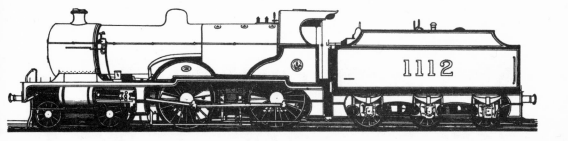

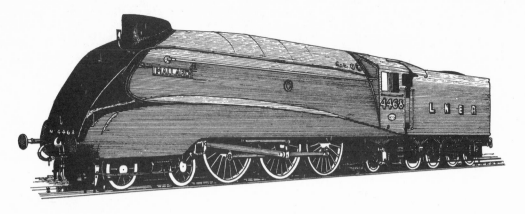

342 LONDON AND NORTH EASTERN RAILWAY 'MALLARD' 1938
Nigel Gresley experimented with streamlining, and in 1935 a casing was built on a new class of Pacifics. These locomotives hauled the east coast expresses to Scotland, and 'Mallard' above, set up a world record of 126 m.p.h. in 1938

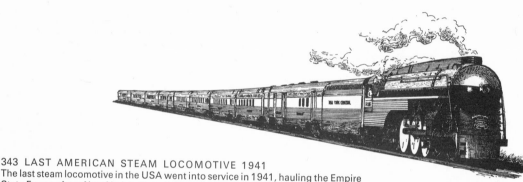

343 LAST AMERICAN STEAM LOCOMOTIVE 1941
The last steam locomotive in the USA went into service in 1941, hauling the Empire State Express from New York to Detroit. The whole train was built of stainless steel, with the locomotive matching the coaches. A 4–6–4 wheel arrangement was used, with solid coupled wheels

344 LAST BRITISH RAILWAYS STEAM LOCOMOTIVE 1960
'Evening Star' was the last steam locomotive built in Britain. It was a standard heavy goods locomotive with ten coupled wheels and two leading bogies. Diesel and electric traction eventually replaced the steam locomotive in this country

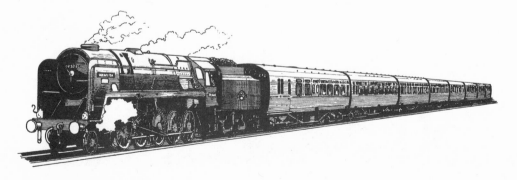

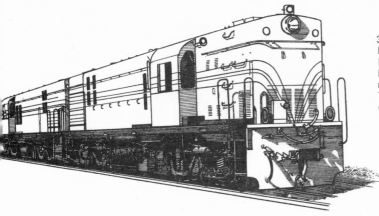

345 GREEK DIESEL LOCOMOTIVES 1960
Massive diesel locomotives for hauling heavy freight trains have replaced the steam locomotive. The picture shows a paired set of diesels belonging to Greek Railways

346 BRITISH RAILWAYS PULLMAN TRAIN 1960
A diesel-electric Pullman train designed for fast, luxurious services from the West Country and the Midlands into London. The train is air conditioned throughout, and is heavily insulated to make it almost noiseless

347 GAS TURBINE LOCOMOTIVE 1965
The Union Pacific Railroad in the USA has always been at the forefront of new development. In the 1960s the company introduced the first gas turbine locomotives

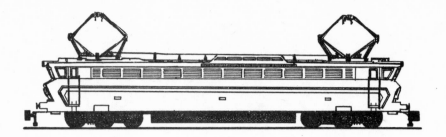

348 EUROPEAN ELECTRIC LOCOMOTIVES 1950s
Pantographs carry the current from overhead wires to power these locomotives. They are a common sight in many European countries, where electrification has gone ahead much quicker than in Britain

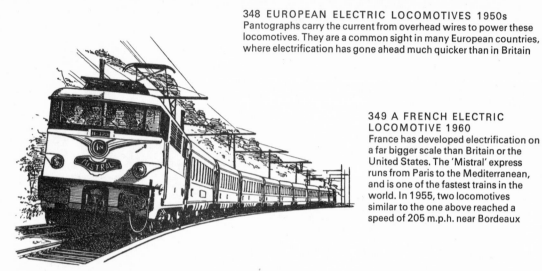

349 A FRENCH ELECTRIC LOCOMOTIVE 1960
France has developed electrification on a far bigger scale than Britain or the United States. The 'Mistral' express runs from Paris to the Mediterranean, and is one of the fastest trains in the world. In 1955, two locomotives similar to the one above reached a speed of 205 m.p.h. near Bordeaux

350 SWISS ELECTRIC LOCOMOTIVE 1969
The availability of cheap electricity meant that Swiss railways were very quickly turned over to electric traction. Because of the mountainous nature of the country, very powerful locomotives have been developed to haul trains. Wonderful feats of bridging and tunnelling carry the railways into the most inaccessible places

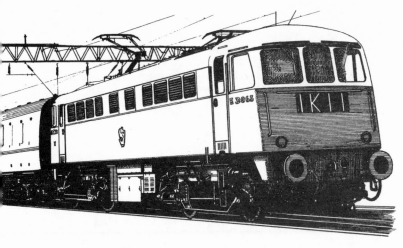

351 BRITISH RAILWAYS ELECTRIC LOCOMOTIVE 1969

These 80 ton locomotives develop 3,300 h.p. and are capable of sustained speeds of up to 100 m.p.h. Current is obtained from overhead wires

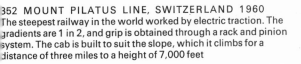

352 MOUNT PILATUS LINE, SWITZERLAND 1960

The steepest railway in the world worked by electric traction. The gradients are 1 in 2, and grip is obtained through a rack and pinion system. The cab is built to suit the slope, which it climbs for a distance of three miles to a height of 7,000 feet

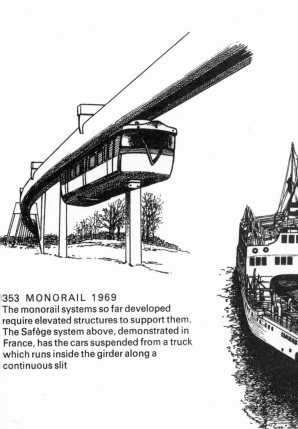

353 MONORAIL 1969

The monorail systems so far developed require elevated structures to support them. The Safège system above, demonstrated in France, has the cars suspended from a truck which runs inside the girder along a continuous slit

354 A TRAIN FERRY 1960s

These useful vessels carry carriages and trucks across stretches of water where bridges are impractical. The ferry above operates across the Straits of Messina between Sicily and the Italian mainland

109

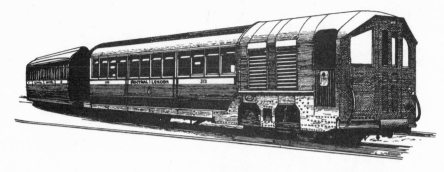

355 LONDON TUBE TRAIN 1907
This was a steel coach built for the City and South London Railway. Good viewing through the large windows was a feature of this new carriage

356 LONDON TUBE TRAIN 1930
This square, rather upright coach was introduced by the London Passenger Transport Board in the 1930s. It was well lit, well appointed, and was fitted with automatic sliding doors

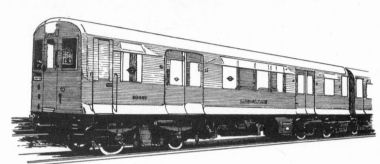

357 LONDON TUBE TRAIN 1969
The familiar squat tube train of the present day was built to suit the tube lines as opposed to the wider tunnel version (figure 356)

358 RAILWAY CARRIAGE 1900
A third class small carriage for short journeys. There are no corridors. The four separate compartments have seats for three passengers each side

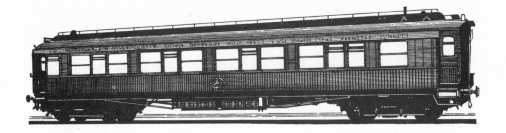

359 A SLEEPING CAR 1900

By the beginning of the twentieth century, sleeping cars, corridor coaches, and restaurant cars had come into use. The Italian sleeping car above was used on long distance express trains. It was lavishly decorated and furnished to cater for the most expensive tastes

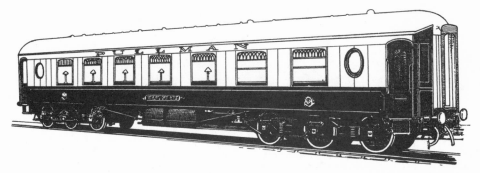

360 A PULLMAN COACH 1911

The American, George Pullman, introduced his elegant carriages in the USA in 1865. Later they were built in England, where they became noted for their comfort. The picture shows a coach used on the London, Brighton and South Coast Railway, with six wheel bogies at each end

361 A CORRIDOR COACH 1950

A post World War II corridor coach, well appointed with good seating and other facilities to make the long journey as comfortable as possible

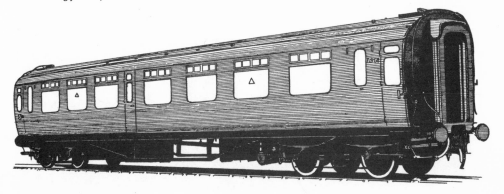

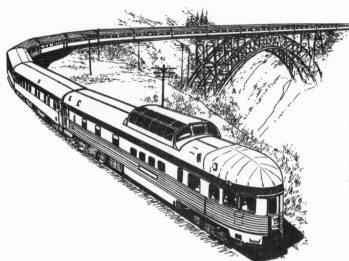

362 A CANADIAN TRANSCONTINENTAL OBSERVATION COACH 1969
This Canadian diesel express is equipped like a travelling hotel for the four-day journey across the Continent. The domed observation car at the rear is one of 16 coaches which make up the train

363 A GOODS WAGGON 1908
These four-wheeled waggons were built mainly to carry coal and other heavy goods. A hand brake only was fitted, as goods trains were not fully braked at this time

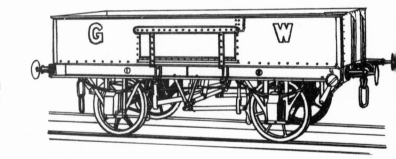

364 AN AMERICAN GRAIN TRUCK 1960s
A 'Big John' grain truck belonging to the United States Southern Railway. The truck can carry 100 tons of grain, and it is fitted with 12 hatches and eight hoppers for rapid loading and unloading

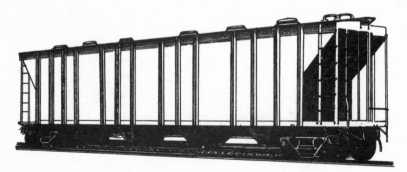

365 THE *MAURETANIA* 1907
The 'Old Lady of the Atlantic' held the Blue Riband for the fastest crossing for 22 years. The four-funnelled giant was driven by four turbine engines which propelled the 32,000 ton ship at a speed of 27 knots. She remained in service until 1934, having been converted to oil burning in 1921

366 THE PANAMA CANAL 1914
Ferdinand de Lesseps planned this canal to cut through the Isthmus of Panama to join the Atlantic to the Pacific. Work began in 1888, but progress was hindered through disease among the workers. The canal was finally opened in 1914. Gigantic locks carry the ships over the hilly sections, and electric locomotives are used to haul ships into the locks

367 THE *NORMANDIE* 1932
The French built this liner to compete with the Germans, Italians, and British on the Atlantic run. She gained the Blue Riband and held it until 1938. During World War II she caught fire in New York and she was broken up in 1946

368 THE *QUEEN MARY* 1934
Launched in 1934, this great ship weighed nearly 82,000 tons when completed. She resembled a floating city, with shops, cinemas, dance halls, and restaurants on board, plus accommodation for 2,000 people.
Four propellers were fitted as well as anti-roll stabilisers to give a smoother passage in rough seas. In 1938 she gained the Blue Riband and held it until 1952. The ship is now out of service and is anchored at Long Beach, California

369 THE *QUEEN ELIZABETH* 1938
The second giant Cunarder was even heavier than her sister, weighing 83,000 tons and driven by steam turbines. She went into service in 1946, having operated as a troopship during World War II. In 1969 she was sold to the USA and is anchored at Everglades, Florida

370 THE *UNITED STATES* 1952
The new type of Atlantic liner which is more economical to run than the *Queens*. The ship is the present holder of the Blue Riband, and is equipped with every modern convenience for passenger comfort

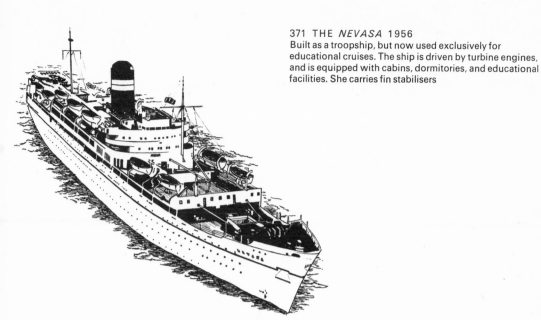

371 THE *NEVASA* 1956
Built as a troopship, but now used exclusively for educational cruises. The ship is driven by turbine engines, and is equipped with cabins, dormitories, and educational facilities. She carries fin stabilisers

372 *LA REINE ASTRIDE* CROSS-CHANNEL SERVICE 1957
This Belgian ship operates the Ostend-Dover route. She is driven by a twin diesel engine and has fin stabilisers, unusual on cross-Channel boats. The ship can carry a thousand passengers in the peak tourist season

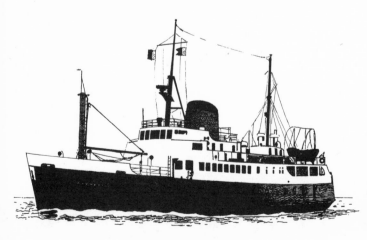

373 THE *CLAYMORE* HIGHLAND FERRY 1955
A modern ferry boat used mainly on the Firth of Clyde. Driven by a twin screw diesel, she weighs just over 1000 tons and can carry up to 500 passengers

374 A TANKER 1950s

The first tanker, the *Gluckhauf,* was launched in 1886, and since that date this type of ship has increased in size. The hull is divided into tanks to carry oil, and the engines are placed aft for safety. Strong construction is necessary because of the stress on a ship of such great length.

375 THE ST. LAWRENCE SEAWAY 1959

This costly undertaking was opened in 1959. A broad canal by-passes rapids, and vessels up to 20,000 tons can now sail right up to Duluth at the Western end of Lake Superior. There are seven sets of locks on the Seaway

376 THE *ROTTERDAM* 1960

An unconventional ship, with twin intakes set towards the stern instead of funnels. Passenger accommodation is classed horizontally through the ship to give maximum freedom of movement to all travellers

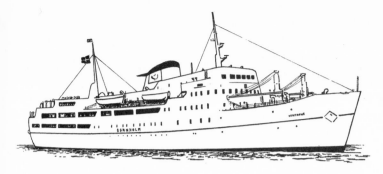

377 THE *BORNHOLM* 1961
This Danish vessel operates in the Baltic as a car ferry. Accommodation is provided for 78 cars which can be driven on and off, as well as for 1800 passengers

378 THE *CANBERRA* 1961
The Peninsular and Orient Line's modern ship has engines placed aft to allow more space for passengers. She is fitted with stabilisers and also with side propellers for better manoeuvring in harbour without tugs

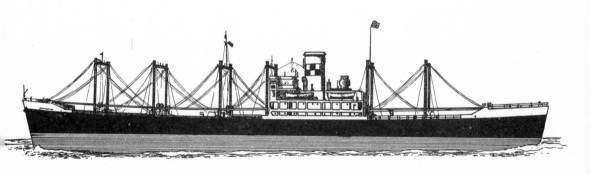

379 A REFRIGERATED SHIP 1960s
The first refrigerated ships went into service in the last quarter of the nineteenth century. They are important for carrying perishable cargoes, in particular frozen meat from Australia, New Zealand, and Argentina

380 A NUCLEAR SUBMARINE 1958
Submarines were the first vessels to be powered by nuclear reactors. The first was the American submarine *Nautilus* in 1955. She travelled submerged below the Polar ice cap, and the voyage raised the interesting possibility of using submarines as the merchant ships of the future

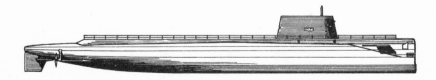

381 THE *SAVANNAH* 1961
This American vessel was the first to go into commercial service using nuclear power. She was essentially an experimental ship, and has proved very costly to run.

382 THE *QUEEN ELIZABETH II* 1969
The Cunard Company ordered this ship to replace the giant *Queens* which were becoming too expensive to run. She is turbine driven and fitted out for luxurious Atlantic crossings as well as for cruises during the winter season

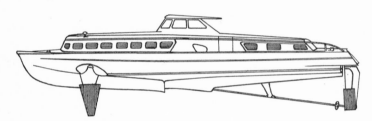

383 A HYDROFOIL 1960s
A new type of ferry which operates in the Channel Islands, from Capri to Sorrento, and in the Baltic Islands. As it gathers speed, the craft rises up at the bow on to skis, which clip the waves as it travels along. The propeller at the stern is set deep in the water

384 A HOVERCRAFT 1960s
Invented by C. S. Cockerell. A fan forces air through slits beneath the craft and forms a cushion of air on which it rides. It is an excellent amphibious craft, and larger versions are being used on cross-Channel services

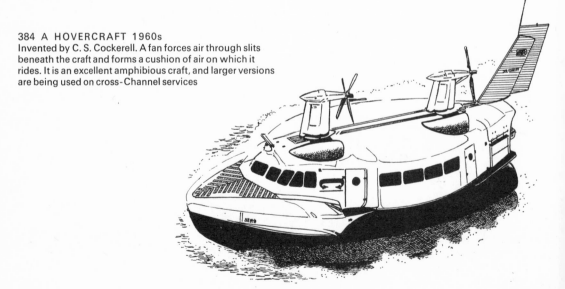

AIR

385 A ZEPPELIN 1900
This rigid airship was 420 feet long and driven by two 16 horse-power engines. Hydrogen filled gas cells were placed inside the framework to give buoyancy

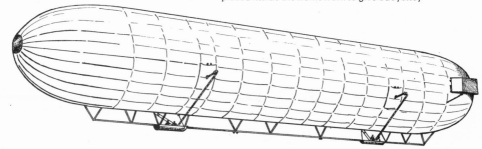

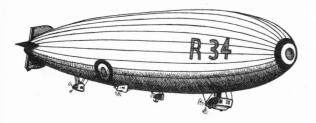

386 THE 'R–34' 1919
This airship made a double crossing of the Atlantic in 1919, the first airship to do so. It was faster than the 'Zeppelins' and was of improved construction

387 THE 'HINDENBURG' 1937
A German airship which operated commercial services across the Atlantic. She carried 50 passengers at a speed of 70 m.p.h. The gas cells were filled with hydrogen rather than the safer helium, and when she caught fire at Lakehurst, New Jersey in 1937, she quickly burnt to ashes and all on board were killed

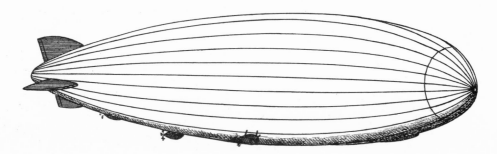

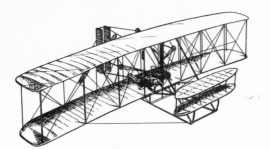

388 THE WRIGHT BIPLANE 1903

The Wright Brothers made the first controlled powered flight in a 'heavier-than-air' machine at Kittyhawk in 1903. The aircraft was a biplane, powered by a 12 h.p. engine. After several flights, they finally achieved a distance of 852 feet, taking 59 seconds

389 SANTOS-DUMONT'S PLANE 1906

This aircraft was the first to fly in Europe. It was a strange machine, which flew tail first, and was built like a box kite

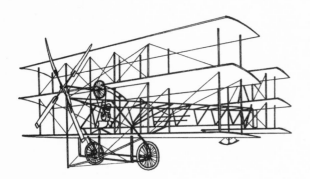

390 A. V. ROE'S PLANE 1909

Roe made the first flight in an all-British aeroplane. The machine was a triplane and was paper covered

391 VOISIN'S PLANE 1909

This French aircraft is notable for the placing of ailerons on the tips of the wings to assist turning

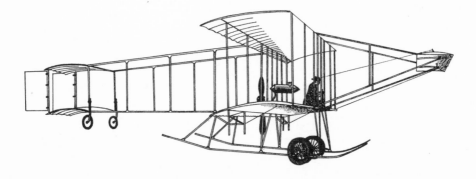

392 BLÉRIOT'S MONOPLANE 1909
With this aircraft Louis Blériot won the prize of £1000 offered by the *Daily Mail* for the first cross-Channel flight. The monoplane construction was unusual at this date. The wings were braced by wires above and below. A 25 h.p. engine drove a two-bladed propeller, and the flight took 37 minutes

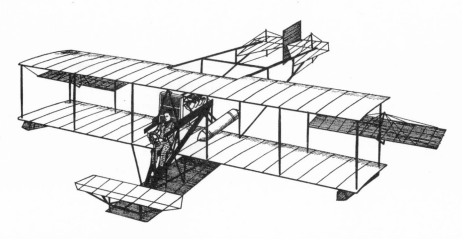

393 A CURTISS SEAPLANE 1912
The American, Glenn Curtiss, made the first seaplane just before the First World War. A pusher motor was fitted between the wings, and the aircraft rested on a central float with balancing floats on each of the wing tips

394 A VICKERS 'VIMY' 1919
John Alcock and Arthur Whitten-Brown made the first non-stop crossing of the Atlantic in this plane in 16 hours. Technical developments in wartime made it possible to consider passenger services by aircraft in the years after 1918

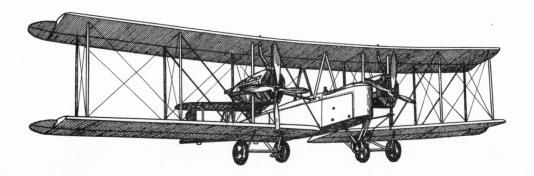

395 CURTISS SEAPLANE 1919
Two American flyers crossed the Atlantic in this machine prior to the flight made by Alcock and Brown. However, they stopped at the Azores on the journey. Their aircraft was a three-engined biplane, with the fuselage shaped like a ship's hull and balance floats on the wing tips

396 A D.H.9 FIGHTER 1919
Military aircraft developed considerably during the war years, and the D.H.9 was a single seater aircraft which could travel well over 100 m.p.h.

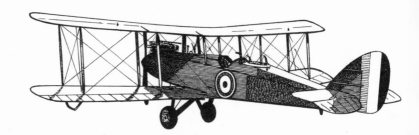

397 AN AUTOGIRO 1923
This machine was developed as a short take off aircraft. The non-powered rotor blades turned as the machine went forward and quickly lifted it off the ground. It was produced in Spain by Juan de La Cierva

398 A FOKKER MONOPLANE 1920s
This Dutch high-wing aircraft was the first all metal plane. It was fitted with three engines and a fixed undercarriage

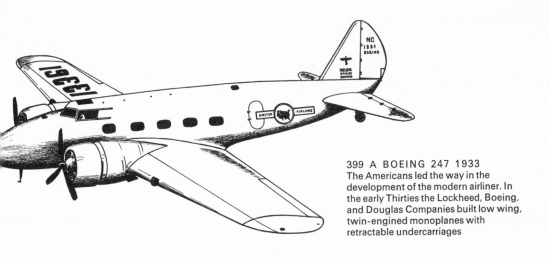

399 A BOEING 247 1933
The Americans led the way in the
development of the modern airliner. In
the early Thirties the Lockheed, Boeing,
and Douglas Companies built low wing,
twin-engined monoplanes with
retractable undercarriages

400 A DOUGLAS DC3 1935
The most widely used air transport in
history, and it is still flying today. The
machine carries up to 30 passengers, and
low running costs make it a useful plane
in many parts of the world

**401 HANDLEY PAGE BIPLANE
1930s**
British Imperial Airways still concentrated
on slow, safe biplanes. These four-
engined aircraft carried 42 people in
great comfort at a cruising speed of just
over 100 m.p.h.

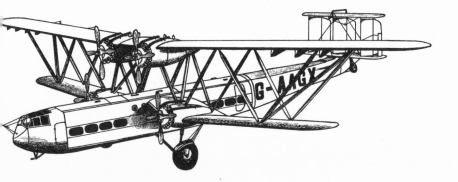

402 SHORT 'EMPIRE' FLYING BOAT 1930s

These aircraft were developed for long distance travel over the sea. Four powerful engines drove the machine along at over 200 m.p.h., and they were used on routes to the Commonwealth and North America in the late Thirties.

403 BOEING 'STRATOCRUISER'

Following World War II the Americans produced long distance airliners to replace the pre-war flying boats. The Boeing 'Stratocruiser' was a low wing, four-engined aircraft which was double-decked. Passengers were accommodated on the upper deck, while below there was a lounge bar and luggage space

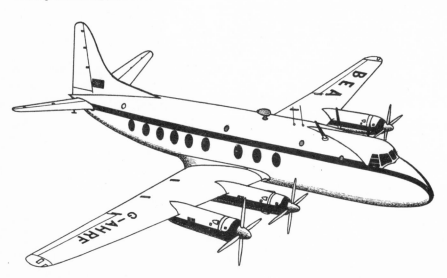

404 VICKERS VISCOUNT TURBO-PROP AIRCRAFT 1953

A very successful short haul aircraft of which over 450 were built. Four Rolls-Royce turbo-prop engines power the plane which is fitted wth pressurised cabins for flying at high altitude

405 A DE HAVILLAND 'COMET' IV 1958

The 'Comet' I was the world's first commercial jet, but unexplained accidents retarded the aircraft's development. However, in 1958 the 'Comet' IV appeared, and became the first jet to fly the Atlantic on a passenger service

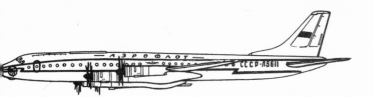

406 RUSSIAN TU 114 1957
At the time of its first flight, this plane was the largest and heaviest aircraft in the world. It was used to operate long distance non-stop services to New York, Havana, and Tokyo

407 FREIGHT PLANE 1960s
A military freight plane, designed to carry a maximum payload of 80,000 lbs. The aircraft has a cruising speed of 350 m.p.h.

408 A RUSSIAN HELICOPTER 1960s
The helicopter, unlike the autogiro (figure 397), has powered rotors. These take the place of wings, and when rotated they lift the machine vertically. Because of this the aircraft can be landed in small spaces

409 A VC10 AIRLINER 1964
This fine looking aircraft is powered by four jet engines mounted below the tail. This allows less vibration and noise in the passenger cabins

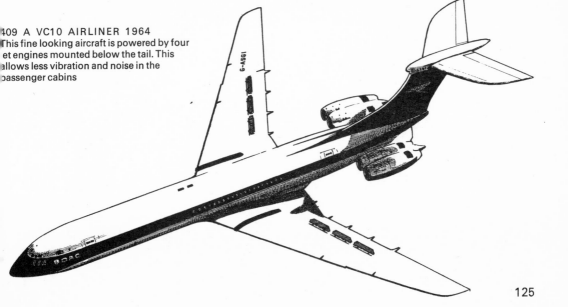

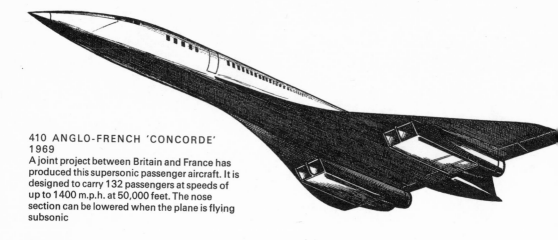

410 ANGLO-FRENCH 'CONCORDE' 1969

A joint project between Britain and France has produced this supersonic passenger aircraft. It is designed to carry 132 passengers at speeds of up to 1400 m.p.h. at 50,000 feet. The nose section can be lowered when the plane is flying subsonic

411 AN AMERICAN ROCKET FOR LAUNCHING SPACE CAPSULES 1960s

The Americans and Russians developed rockets based on the German V2 at the end of World War II. Eventually they were made powerful enough to put satellites, and later space craft, into orbit round the earth. The American 'Saturn' rockets are fired from the base at Cape Kennedy in Florida

412 AN AMERICAN SPACE CAPSULE 1960s

During the last ten years the Americans have put capsules into space as part of a long-term programme which aims to explore many of the planets in the Solar System. Those manned by astronauts have orbited the Earth while the men have carried out various experiments such as the 'space-walking' below. The fruits of this work were realised in 1969 when the first men landed on the Moon from the 'Apollo' spaceships

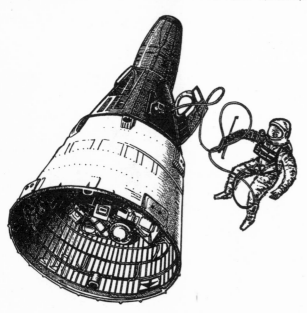

General Index

Index of Persons